# ALBA EMOTING:
# A SCIENTIFIC METHOD FOR EMOTIONAL INDUCTION

## SUSANA BLOCH

*Alba Emoting: A Scientific Method for Emotional Induction*
Copyright © 2015 by Susana Bloch. All rights reserved.

No part of this publication can be reproduced or transmitted in any form or by any means, electronic or mechanical, without permission in writing from the author or publisher.

*Alba Emoting: A Scientific Method for Emotional Induction* by Susana Bloch
Cover design by Maggie Cousins
Book design by Rob Siders, 52 Novels

*Al Alba de las Emociones*, 1st published in Spanish 2002,
by Editorial Grijalbo (Random House Mondadori).
Re-edited in 2007 by Uqbar Editores
Re-released in 2015

Translation into English by the Author first published as *The Alba of Emotions*, Ediciones Ultramarinos PSE, 2006 (Santiago, Chile).

Second revised edition,
Edited by Patricia Angelin and Elizabeth Ann Townsend
2017

Copyright © 2017 Susana Bloch

To my daughters, Alejandra and Claudia,
here and There

# CONTENTS

PROLOGUE by Pedro Sándor — 9

PREFACE by Patricia Angelin — 15

THE AUTHOR CONVERSES WITH HER FRIENDS — 19

**PART I**
**THE SPACE OF *ALBA EMOTING*** — 27
   What is *Alba Emoting*? — 29

I. AROUND THE SUBJECT OF EMOTIONS — 31
   Why and how I got interested in the subject of emotions — 31
   Neuroscience, Theatre and Emotions — 32
   Why and how do we emote? — 35
   The emotional state — 38
   The study of emotions: A psychophysiological approach — 42
   Definition and analysis of an emotion — 42
   Three levels of activation — 45
   William James: The James-Lange Theory — 49
   Basic emotions — 52
   Is the subjective experience of a basic emotion the same for everyone? — 56
   From basic emotions to mixed emotions — 58
      *Intensity and duration of an emotional state* — 60
      *Mixed Emotions* — 63

II. EXPERIENTIAL REPORTS — 67

## III. PUBLISH OR PERISH — 76
Leaving Chile across the Andes — 77
In Paris, by the Seine river — 79
Measuring respiratory rhythms — 81
Dramatic adieu to the pigeon world — 82
Structured representation of the basic emotions — 85
The observer recognizes what he sees: Is such judgment valid? — 86
Analysis of the subjective content of an emotion — 87
Publishing in *Theatre Topics* — 88
The article in *Science & Vie* — 89

# PART II
# SCIENCE AND EMOTION — 91

## I. SCIENTIFIC FOUNDATIONS: DISCOVERING THE EMOTIONAL EFFECTOR PATTERNS — 95
First empirical observations — 95
Experiences and recordings under hypnosis — 97
We feel what we breathe — 101
*How do we breathe these basic emotions?* — 101
Body posture and facial expression — 103
*How does the body move in different emotional states?* — 104
*What happens with our faces when we emote?* — 106

## II. THE EMOTIONAL EFFECTOR PATTERNS — 108
Respiratory-postural-facial patterns — 108
Neutral (non–emotional breathing) — 117

## III. *ALBA EMOTING:* A NEW METHOD FOR EMOTIONAL INDUCTION — 119
Emotional induction: procedure to "enter" into an emotion — 119
The "Step-Out" procedure — 124
From the technique to the method: Recommendations to learn *Alba Emoting* — 127

## PART III
## ADVENTURES OF THE AUTHOR WITH HER METHOD    131

I. IN THE THEATRE WORLD    133
   Stories lived with theatre people    133
   Training actors    138
      *The basic emotional patterns*    139
      *Modulation of intensity*    141
      *Succession of emotional patterns and theatre games*    141
      *The "Step-Out" technique*    144
      *Mixed Emotions*    145
      *Analysis and notation of the "emotional melodies" of dramatic texts*    146
      *Collateral Psychotherapeutic Effects*    147
      *Resistance to the use of the method: defenders and detractors*    148
   Conclusions for training actors    151

II. IN THE FILM WORLD WITH PEDRO SÁNDOR    153

III. OPENING TO OTHER DOMAINS OF ACTION    158
   Publicity    154
   Organizational Development    160
   Psychotherapy    162

FINAL COMMENTS    167
   Final Words of the Author to this Second Revised Edition    173
   Elizabeth Ann Townsend    174
   Patricia Angelin    177

EPILOGUE    181

APPENDIX I
SPECIFIC RESPIRATORY PATTERNS DISTINGUISH
AMONG HUMAN BASIC EMOTIONS    183

APPENDIX II
THE SCRIPT OF THE ALBA EMOTING FILM    211

ACKNOWLEDGMENTS    223

# PROLOGUE BY PEDRO SÁNDOR

*For big evils, great remedies*

We need to isolate and express intensely the basic emotions in order to better recognize and understand our ever present mixed emotions, the incredible sublime emotions, and our exasperating moods, with their sequels – altered psychological states such as stress, induced disorientation, depression, schizophrenia and others.

The rapid developments of metropolis replacing countryside, a more and more sedentary daily life, the culture-shock of television, virtual worlds, the speed of technological changes, the globalization of economies and cultures, and the accelerated deterioration of the ecological niche, all produce a loss of our capacity to feel and express emotions,

The mechanical language of machines that have no emotions predominates over human presence, which is essentially emotional.

Our modernity, with its huge mechanistic invasion overpowering what is human, confuses and reduces the physical expression of emotional codes, which are essential for the survival of our species.

We are faced with a critical question. Can the noise of machines recoil and disappear in the face of the divine sonority of human emotional expression?

**Alba Emoting** is a system that, starting from particular ways of breathing followed by simple physical actions, makes it possible to feel and express the emotions of *sadness, joy, fear, anger, sexuality,* and *tenderness* in all their strength and purity. It is a great remedy for recovering the lost dimension of emoting.

Susana Bloch calls these six emotions, "basic emotions."

To experience the expressive strength of these basic emotions makes it possible for us to have a better perception of the emotional rhythms and melodies that fill our daily living spaces and thus enter into our own emotional rhythms and melodies more naturally.

At the same time, appreciation of the truly real emotional silence which is produced in the rarely attained neutral emotional states, increases. This silence occurs occasionally and usually suddenly and, when it happens, we say, "an angel just passed by." This is a state of meditation that is essential for emotional balance.

The style in which this book is written is unusual; it strives to communicate the essential role emotions play in the quality of life of human beings, especially in the vertigo of this present time.

This is a narrative style that Susana developed when she worked with me on the film, called *Alba Emoting*, a style which she continued to use later in her book, *Biology of Emotions and Alba Emoting, Dancing Together*, written jointly with the Chilean biologist, Humberto Maturana, in 1996.

Susana lets her writing flow, driven by her need to communicate with the reader, almost like the child she once was, full of imagination when in the presence of the songs of birds, rivers, sand and air, and above all, of laughter, sorrow, tenderness, anger, erotic love and human fear.

To allow herself to flow in this writing as a child, being in fact a woman of a certain age, implies an act of wise maturity. Otherwise, the coherence and specific intellectual stature of **Alba Emoting** could not have been transmitted.

With the unexpected structure of this book, which appears to be almost naïve, with non-linear timing, intermingling testimonials, poems and sentences that are significant to her, the author succeeds in transmitting the enormous complexity that lies behind an apparently simple technique, and avoids a mechanistic transmission of de-emotionalized knowledge and experience, without sacrificing the rigor and clarity needed to communicate this important scientific discovery. Her discovery deals with the "Emotional Effector Patterns" of *sadness, joy, anger, fear, sexuality,* and *tenderness.*

These patterns are the same for all human beings, independent of their cultural origins, physical characteristics or geographical locations. They are biological, non-psychological and non-historical.

The system created on the basis of this discovery was named ***Alba Emoting*** by its authors, Susana Bloch and myself.

The reader of this book, who wishes to enter more rapidly into the subject matter, should begin with Part II and then go on to Appendix I.

To those readers who want to understand more subtly and in depth the richness, power and complexity involved in the use of this method, – which goes far beyond a mere mechanical reproduction of the Emotional Effector Patterns– I recommend that this book be read from beginning to end.

I invite you to journey with Susana through the intricacies of her mind, heart, soul, and personality that brought her to discover a great secret hidden since the dawn of time, in the depths of the most profound and inscrutable chest of mysteries.

I, as her friend and partner in so many adventures, under different suns, moons, winds, and rains, share this free spirit of Susana's.

She has asked me to write this Prologue, which is for me an atavistic, spiritual and poetic privilege, so I end it with a poem written 'clamus correnti', as the pen runs:

## SOY

*De luz y sombra*
*de certezas y dudas*
*mas allá de todo acto de cordura.*

*Vorágine sensorial*
*cuerpo abandonado*
*Psiquis solitaria*

*Solo*
*todo solo,*
*solo*
*hasta el Final.*

*Un hombre solo*
*En medio*
*de un universo destructor*
*de la belleza salvaje*
*emocional,*
*animal*
*vegetal*
*mineral-*

SOY

Pedro Sándor
7 de Enero del 2002
La Reina, Santiago
Chile

## I AM

Of light and shadow
of certitudes and doubts
beyond any act of judiciousness.

Sensorial turmoil
Abandoned body
Solitary psyche

Alone
All alone
Alone until the End.

A man alone
In the midst of a destructive universe
Of the savage beauty
emotional
animal
vegetable
mineral-

I AM

                        Four o'clock in the morning
                        Of a summer night
                        Fresh, moreover romantic
                        And I alone in the depth of
                        the ocean
                        Alone, over there, far beyond.

# PREFACE
# BY PATRICIA ANGELIN

I approach this book with "fear and trembling." How do I *know* my emotional state? Easy answer: Dr. Susana Bloch and her **Alba Emoting**. Because of her revolutionary gift to the world, I am empowered to observe my fear in-the-moment with clarity. In my body is a complex mixture composed of several intense feelings:

- That initial desire to run away, to avoid, to hide away in the face of this huge Work (capitalization intended) of Susana;
- A deeper oceanic tenderness, as embracing—but neither holding nor clinging—as the edenic inlet of the Pacific Ocean, *Las Cujas*, at Dr. Bloch's country retreat in Cachagua, Chile;
- A touch of sadness, that further relaxes tensed muscles, due to the impossibility of conveying to you the honor and respect due to this scientist (who possesses the soul of an artist) for this effective tool of affective knowledge of Self and Other;
- A hint of erotic, not in the sexual sense, but in the wonder-filled pleasure of opening up to her great heart and mind;
- Joy for the adventure ahead—it makes me giddy and gleeful in childlike anticipation!
- Finally there is anger—yes, anger—which followed quickly upon my initial recognition of fear. And this tiny propulsion of anger moved me forward to write this Foreword.

Of course, the above happened in a Nano-second and took much longer to express in words, while cognitively analyzing the occurrence.

So… entirely because of **Alba Emoting** I [*Who*] know *what* I feel, *where* it is placed in my body, *how* it got there, and the precise *when* progression of the emotion(s). Wow. Freedom. Freedom to make decisions; Freedom from bondage to my own emotional reactivity; Freedom to "be me" in the fuller sense. I need not repress… although I am free to suppress if appropriate. I am so grateful for the wholeness, I beg you to indulge me in a literary flight of fancy:

*Once upon a time there was a lovely scientist. Born in Europe just before a world cataclysm, reared in South America… a daughter of two worlds, old and new. She loved adventures of the mind and the heart and the body.*

*Janus-headed, she looked to art and then to science, both.*

*Accepting her duality, she embraced pure science.*

*But…when one gives freely of oneself, one eventually recovers oneself again in wholeness: From pure science…working with artists as "naïve subjects"…the lovely scientist recovered the other part of herself. She embraced Eros passionately in a union of science and art…The artist-scientist became wholly herself.*

Artists are often the first to occupy new spaces. We come before anyone has "heard of" the neighborhood. We come when it is still dangerous to live and work there. Then, because the artists are established… gradually people in general start to notice. Carefully, watchfully, cautiously they too move in… and there is "gentrification."

So it was and is with **Alba Emoting**: Susana Bloch and her actors go in, fearlessly, first. The rest of the world will follow.

A final note to you, dear Reader: This book is creative. It can be read visually. Perhaps you will wish to go through once, reading only what is in Italics; then go through again, reading only what Dr. Bloch has written in Bold; then to go through looking at her illustrations; and only then to engage the order she has chosen for the non-linear exposition of her thought. Please feel free. Susana Bloch will be delighted for you to engage her quicksilver thought as you wish. You are about to begin an encounter with a genuinely original mind.

I am so grateful, and make a mental obeisance, curtseying to the ground, to artist-scientist Susana Bloch. You may have read Constantin Stanislavsky's *My Life in Art*? This book could be entitled, *My Life in Science and Art*, by Susana Bloch. Long may she grace this world with her mercurial, scintillating presence.

As Pedro Sándor says to Susana: *Coraje y al toro! (Courage! At the Bull!)*

**Patricia Angelin
New York City, NY,
USA**

From Left To Right: Patricia Angelin, Pedro Sándor, Susana Bloch

# THE AUTHOR CONVERSES WITH HER FRIENDS

*Leaves of fire entangled in my hair*

*Sun shining out from my hair, and spreading into the sea*

*I tremble in front of Beauty*

J oanna, my friend, said to me:

"*In Paris I met a lady with a huge smile under a big hat: she works with emotions, studies them, turns them around, looks at them, bewitches them!*"

That is I.

And my friend Pedro says,

"*You can write this book in one second because it comes to you as a gift from time immemorial. You already carry it written in you,*" and ends with his usual ¡*Coraje y al toro!* (Courage and face the bull!) with which he decisively pushes me into the arena.

So I leap with all my being into writing this book as creatively as possible, leaving behind the academic constraints from so many years of publishing in the scientific world.

I begin to fly freely, in order to tell you about this adventure that deals with the story of scientific research that discovered the passionate love affair existing between breathing and emotion, and resulted in describing the "Emotional Effector Patterns" of the basic emotions:

### *Joy, Sadness, Anger, Fear, Sexuality, Tenderness*

I invite all of you to enter with me into the inscrutable, mysterious and powerful universe of BASIC EMOTIONS, the knowledge of which enables us to understand MIXED EMOTIONS, MOODS and HIGHER EMOTIONS in another, clearer way.

The rest… is silence…

Suddenly, from this silence, I listen to the breath of the emotions and get submerged in the air and rain they bring, and I wish to share with you the unrest I felt venturing into the process of discovering ***Alba Emoting.***

**What most impresses about emotions in general is how invasive and dominant they are, how they install themselves rapidly and change from one to another with the speed of the wind and the violence of lightning, how they forever occupy an essential role in our lives, taking root everlastingly in our human condition —all this without the slightest intervention of our will.**

When this reflection entered into the depth of my being, the decision to investigate became imperative: to grasp emotions, tame them, smell, taste and dissect them...

But at the same time doubts arose and I felt unsure about daring to plunge into them. Because of their magnitude and violence, I might find myself overwhelmed in excessively complex emotional dimensions.

And I remember Aunt Veronica, who from the pages of Angeles Mastretta's book *"Mujeres de Ojos Grandes" (Women with Big Eyes)* says:

*"Todo menos desgobernar la máquina de las pasiones,*
*con esa es mejor no meterse"*
*"Anything but misgovern the machine of passions.*
*Better not to meddle with those."*

Things being as they are, would I be capable of persevering in this venture without dismay, without desertion?

At that precise moment a poem by Pedro Sándor entitled *Piel de Mujer* (Woman Skin), which I felt approached the subject with great lucidity, appeared, allowing me to face this conflict.

Here is the poem:

### *Piel de Mujer*

*Penetro tranquilamente en la
profundidad de mi piel.*

*A ver quién se atreve a penetrar
tranquilamente, lúcidamente en la profundidad de su piel.
Nadie, sólo yo.*

*Renunciar a todos los mitos,
todas las creencias, confiar
en el latido del ritual de la vida,
escondida, vibrante, poderosa
en la profundidad de la piel.*

*A ver quién se atreve.
Nadie, sólo yo.*

*Hay que tener coraje para penetrar
lúcidamente bajo su piel,
sin desmayos, sin abandonos,
ante la vorágine torrentosa de sangre azul
de las pasiones milenarias,
que laten y circulan en oleadas gigantescas,
bajo la piel.*

*Primero la Pasión, luego la Razón,
en un movimiento cadencioso perfecto
organizado, dirigido, controlado,
desatado en mi,
por tu Piel de Mujer.*

### *Woman Skin*

I calmly penetrate
Into the depth of my skin.

Who dares to penetrate
Calmly, lucidly
Into the depth of their skin?

No one, only I.

To renounce all myths,
All beliefs, to trust the pulse of life's ritual,
Hidden, vibrant, powerful,
In the depths of our skin.

Who dares,
No one, only I.

One needs courage to penetrate
Lucidly under one's skin
Without faltering, without desertion,
In the face of the stormy turmoil of blue blood
Of ancient passions
That pulse and circulate in gigantic waves
Under the skin.

First Passion, then Reason
In a perfect rhythmic movement
Organized, directed, controlled,
Unchained in me
By your Woman Skin.

I therefore accepted the challenge to enter into the emotions, sustained by this masculine poetic reflection.

**Let us recognize, modulate and express the basic emotions, feeling them, dignifying them, and recovering their absolute biological origin and their universal significance.**

And finally, coincidentally, unexpectedly, almost prophetically -as if brought by a whirlwind- these verses of a popular Chilean song reached me:

> *Yo me enamoré del aire, aire, aire*
> *y en el aire aire yo me quede.*
>
> *Bonito es el aire pero quien podrá*
> *Detener su marcha su rumbo fijar*
>
> *Bonito es el aire pero quien podrá*
> *Detener su marcha su rumbo final.*

> I fell in love with the air, air, air
> and in the air, air I stayed
>
> Lovely is the air, but who could stop its path,
> fix its direction?
>
> Lovely is the air, but who could stop its path,
> its final destination.

(free translation by the author)

# PART I
# THE SPACE OF *ALBA EMOTING*

# WHAT IS ALBA EMOTING?

*Alba Emoting*™ is a method that allows people to connect physically with their emotions, through special breathing patterns, accompanied by postural attitudes and facial expressions. The awareness of these precise respiratory, postural, and facial actions help people to express, recognize, and modulate their emotions creatively, to better recognize them in others, and to transmit them without ambiguity.

The method, based on scientific findings, permits anyone to enter into the complex world of emotions, by learning to reproduce at will these specific respiratory-postural-facial patterns typical of each basic emotion, as scientifically determined.

This is the entry into the *Alba Emoting* System.

# I. AROUND THE SUBJECT OF EMOTIONS

The *racconto* or story in the following pages is not presented in linear form or in chronological order, but rather as a blending of thoughts, sensations, and poetic expressions, mixed with concrete facts, autobiographical notes and scientific experiments, all of which have traced the direction of my ventures in walking and feeling around this world.

This kind of *racconto* has a narrative structure that is intellectually, emotionally and physically attractive to me.

## WHY AND HOW I GOT INTERESTED IN THE SUBJECT OF EMOTIONS

I have always had a variety of strong simultaneous interests. At school it was athletics in the mornings and literature in the afternoons. Later it was theatre, psychology and neuroscience. I am a Gemini, always doing several things at the same time. It is difficult for me to stay inactive or in a contemplative mood. That's the story of my life and perhaps explains my style of living and writing.

> When I finished High School I had to choose between theatre and psychology. I was attracted to theatre already as a child, and began writing scripts inspired by the soap operas I listened to on the radio without my German mother's permission. Years later, after a successful audition at the Drama School of the University of Chile, I remember my terror at initiating a career in which often actors identified so intensely with their characters' emotions that they could become unbalanced in their lives.
>
> Fear won over passion and I ran away from the Drama Department and rapidly registered in the Psychology Department, where

after a strict selection, I was admitted as a regular student. My interests were centered right from the beginning on the relationship between biology and psychology, so I specialized in brain function, both in research and in teaching. My passion for the theatre remained dormant, but ready to emerge at the first opportunity.

Looking back at my entire life I realize that I always travel along paths full of brilliant colors, forms and rhythms. In the professional realm it was first the theatre and the emotions, then twenty long years doing basic research with pigeons and other animals, finally leaving those areas in order to concentrate exclusively on human emotion. And, as a result of having had a long research career, this interest resulted in the creation of the *Alba Emoting* System.

Another of my characteristics is to return to the beginning. In fact, *Alba Emoting* is, among other things, a method that precisely protects the actor from that which I so much feared in my teens, and which drove me away from the theatre: the strong identification many actors had with their characters' emotions, which often adversely affected their private lives.

It may well be that I have completed many years of scientific research on emotions just in order to discover a method which allows anyone —not just actors as we shall see later- **to call up an emotion, and to learn to leave it at will, by means of precisely controlled physical actions.**

## NEUROSCIENCE, THEATRE AND EMOTIONS

In the year 1970, I was Full Professor of Neurophysiology in the Psychology Department, and Associate Professor of Neurophysiology at the Department of Physiology in the School of Medicine, both positions at the University of Chile, in Santiago.

At that time, I received an unexpected invitation from the Theatre School of the same University to teach psychology to their students. It was a novelty that a psychologist not involved in clinical work or in pedagogical counseling, but rather specialized in experimental psychophysiology and in basic research with animal subjects, should be invited to work with actors. It was certainly an unusual collaboration in those days. But in Chile we are often unacknowledged pioneers and innovators in different areas of knowledge.

So, I was invited to a meeting with the full teaching staff of the Theatre Department to discuss their proposal. In the midst of a lively interaction I was suddenly magically inspired and daringly proposed that instead of a theoretical course in Psychology, it could be far more interesting to create an **experimental workshop for the study of emotions, with an interdisciplinary collaboration between scientists and theatre experts.**

It was certainly quite an unusual proposition, though so attractive, that Pedro Orthous, one of the best Chilean theatre directors and professors of the School, immediately reacted with great enthusiasm expressing his wish to be part of such a venture. And so he was.

I came back to my laboratory quite excited and shared the idea with my colleague, Guy Santibáñez-H. We started immediately to design a research project on the study of human emotions.

And so, as life unfolds, the research that I then began on the subject of human emotions and my love for the theatre was in fact triggered by that unexpected, and perhaps predestined, invitation!

We had already collaborated with Guy on many experiments in animal psychophysiology, such as neural mechanisms in learning processes, and the role of motivation in behavior. In those years neuroscience was developing rapidly in our country and we had good training and experience in the area. Most of us had specialized abroad, and we had continuous contact with the best neurophysiologists in the world at that time.

*I vividly remember how impressed we young researchers were, how eager to learn at those meetings held regularly in Santiago at the home of Joaquin Luco, a great Chilean professor and scientist. How attentively we listened to the talks of both Chilean and notable foreign scientists, accompanied by the delicious appetizers prepared by Joaquin Luco's wife, Doña Ines!*

So the beginning of the experimental work on emotions, which produced the embryo of the "Emotional Effector Patterns," and the first glimpses that led later to the creation of the ***Alba Emoting*** System, was a collaborative work with Guy Santibañez and Pedro Orthous.

Then came the 1973 military *coup d'état* in Chile; we dispersed and that was the end of our collaboration.

Since then I have continued the scientific research on the relation between breathing and emotion, which provided a framework for the initial embryo. I developed many studies of increasing complexity based on those initial experiments with other collaborators in my laboratory in Paris. In this way the system we later named **Alba Emoting** grew from a solid scientific foundation.

At the same time I was able quietly to continue working with the method in the theatre, in collaboration with Horacio Muñoz, a very talented and creative Chilean theater director and close friend, who at that time was living and directing in Denmark. I traveled to Copenhagen in my spare time, and we created there a Center for Theatre investigation, experimenting with his actors, and developing new applications of the method.

**During all these years Alba Emoting has spread widely internationally, continuously enlarging its field of action. It has evoked keen interest in other areas such as Psychotherapy, Education, Health, Sports, Publicity, Business, and other enterprises, all involved with communication, human relations and emotional health.**

In all this my friend Pedro Sándor, co-creator of the **Alba Emoting** System, has played a fundamental role in extending the application of the "Emotional Effector Patterns." In quite a special way, which is difficult to explain, his participation in my work has been essential. He foresaw from the very beginning the vast potential our experiments had as a concrete physical tool for harnessing the power of emotions in any area of human endeavor. He helped me to develop a theoretical framework for our experimental findings, placing them in a much wider perspective as he foresaw the power **Alba Emoting** had for humanity.

**One may wonder at this point of the racconto—what is the relationship between my passion for the theatre and my study of emotions? This is quite simple. An actor is, in the words of Antonin Artaud– the genial French poet and man of the theatre– an "athlete of emotions." Undoubtedly, therefore, actors are ideal subjects for studying emotions.**

In fact, when doing research, scientists always choose the optimal experimental subjects for their studies. If, for instance, a biophysicist wants to analyze the mechanisms of nerve conduction, it is best for him to record from an animal possessing the largest nerve fibers possible, like those from the giant squid. If however his scientific interests concern color vision, he

## WHY AND HOW DO WE EMOTE?

> I am passing by a small square where I spent part of my adolescence, and I see a bench, which reminds me of my very first flirtations. I am driving around in search of a nice house for rent; I am slightly irritated, as I cannot find an adequate one for my budget. Suddenly the sight of that bench brings me back into my past. I smile slightly and as the memory becomes more intense, with some concrete images, I may even blush at the memory, my heart beating faster.

It is also possible that the same bench could evoke a sad memory in someone else, such as having broken up with a lover there. So the same external stimulus will trigger different memories, and therefore different emotional reactions, according to the history or present circumstances of the person.

Another possibility is that at the same moment that we are evoking a tender memory, our car is hit from behind. We jump out in fury to insult the driver, who turns out to be a dear old friend. We have not seen each other for a long time, and our anger is instantly transformed into joy and we hug each other.

All this may happen in just a few seconds.

How fluctuating are our thoughts and our feelings! We even rebel and say, "No this would never happen to me. I am aware of my emotions." The real concrete fact is that we are continuously subject to such emotional drifting. In the cases just mentioned, the different emotional states or emotional reactions may be triggered by a real stimulus, as in the case of the car being hit, or result from the memory of a situation evoked by the view of an object associated with a past experience (for example, the bench). In literature such an emotional association is perfectly exemplified in the famous tea aroma with the *madeleines* (cookies) which evoke a cascade of memories in Marcel Proust's character from the novel *In Search of the lost Time*, or *Remembrance of Things Past*.

This brings to my mind some lines of a poem by Paul Verlaine:

*Les sanglots longues, des violons, de l'automne*
*Blessent mon coeur d'une langueur monotone.*

The long autumn wails, like violins,
Wounding my heart in a languid monotone.

(Author's translation)

And the emotions flow freely. In the case of the slight car collision, our reaction is violent, quite primitive and universal. It is a reaction to an aggression that bursts out very rapidly, without thought. Our movements become abrupt —we literally jump out of the car with a hard look, and an ugly frown, a shrieking voice and an accelerated breathing. This is usually a brief instant in which our human behavior does not differ much from that of an infuriated beast!

Yes, so it is. If we are honest, we must agree that we become ugly creatures —or at least what is conventionally considered "ugly"— even if probably a second later our cultural, educational, or ethnic training will temper our initial reaction.

I remember a film done by the French filmmaker, Alain Resnais together with the French biologist, Henri Laborit, called *Mon Oncle en Amerique*. In the film, human couples appear discussing and fighting in a manner quite similar to the behavior of rats in the laboratory when they attack each other or when they show panic reactions. To make the similarity more evident in the artistic cinematographic creation, the humans shown arguing, though dressed normally as humans, carry hoods with painted rat features.

I commented on the film at a dinner with a psychiatrist who was furious with the comparison. I would say that we often behave as animals and that only our consciousness and the other poles of our human nature—spiritual and cultural—give us the chance to control ourselves and transcend behaviors that we consider *a posteriori* quite abominable, but from which it is often hard to escape.

We know nowadays that there is a special region in our brain – the amygdala, a tiny structure, part of the limbic system situated in the midbrain– which has direct connections with the muscles, and which is responsible for the swiftness and abruptness of the above mentioned emotional reactions since it allows commands for actions to go directly to the effectors (the muscles that will execute the physical actions) bypassing the cerebral cortex.

This means that there is no time for thinking, for processing information, which is very important when an instant reaction is required, as for instance when facing a danger.

Joseph Le Doux, a North American neurophysiologist who has investigated the physiological basis of fear, postulates that early fears in a very young child are probably registered in this tiny brain structure.

In the case of the memories evoked by the bench in the small square, described above, the reaction is more subtle and internal. Nevertheless it will express itself externally by a sudden change in the direction of the gaze, a break in the sound of the voice, a slight blush in the cheeks, all signs, however small, that would signal to a careful observer that there has been a change in the person's emotional state, and explain a sudden shift from small talk to a moment of silence and withdrawal. The observer might even be able to identify whether the memory evoked by that person is sad, erotic, or simply funny.

And the observer may perceive all this without having exchanged a single word!

> *I listen to Chopin on my old portable cassette player; it is infallible that even at the first chords of the theme, tears which I cannot control will come to my eyes. I look out the window perceiving the dusky sea atmosphere. My soul lifts as my fingers play on the keyboard of my small computer as if they were interpreting on the piano that remarkable Nocturne my friend had recorded some time ago to accompany me during a long illness... I feel the silence outside, the fading light, the variety of bushes and trees in the wide quiet road outside my beach house. My friend lives under the eucalyptus tree across the dusty road. Sometimes we meet in the center of the road and we chat, oh, we chat so much. What joy! I remember another friend who once advised me to buy a particular musical interpretation because it was so beautiful that it "hurt."*

A whole stream of images flow from my own emotions.

Another way of initiating or modifying an emotional state may occur in response to a simple sensation: a stomach cramp or a speeding of the heart rate makes one think of a possible disease and we become anxious.

Or the feeling of warmth on the skin under the sun provokes a pleasant feeling of wellbeing, which is close to joy. It is also possible to modify our emotional flow with thoughts, fantasies or daydreams.

The fact is that willy-nilly we are continuously oscillating among emotional states having different degrees of intensity or duration. Such fluctuations in mood are essentially not under voluntary control. Sad memories come to our minds: we try to expel them, but they are stubborn. We do not want to think about someone, but the mind is insistent and does not give in.

The most difficult thing is to clear the mind of all sorts of images, and thoughts, what we colloquially call "stopping the mind." Otherwise, one way or the other we become slaves to these continuous mental shifts.

That is why one needs to learn how to meditate.

## THE EMOTIONAL STATE

What is an emotion? A state of mind? A state of the soul? A physical sensation, a blush on the face, a faster heartbeat, an anxious oppression in the chest, a pair of languid eyes? An emotion is all of this and much more. It is very difficult to define precisely.

People generally say that they are "moved" when they have a strong impression, a sort of excitation, but it is usually only in reference to certain emotional states, for example a great joy, a deep sorrow or a melancholic blending of both. "*When I saw my daughter descending from the plane after a long absence, I was so moved that I began to cry,*" or "*I was very moved when my son won that prize at the Olympics,*" or "*When I had my newborn in my arms, it moved me to see how fragile she was.*"

Curiously enough when we are angry or anxious or sexually aroused, we do not say that "we are moved."

How do we get to recognize what emotional state we are in?

Quite often we do not see it ourselves, although it is evident to the observer. "*Why have you become so angry?*" asks the young waiter who has politely served me coffee. "*I am not angry,*" I respond angrily, unaware of the expression of disgust reflected on my face or the way I have brusquely handled the cup of coffee.

These non-verbal expressions, of which we are mostly unaware, may be perfectly clear and unequivocal for the other. This means that intentionally or not, such emotional signals **always** communicate something, even if the communication is totally non-verbal.

This mode of communicating, technically called "paralinguistic," is in many cases more salient than the cognitive content of the words. Moreover, it may be in total disagreement with what is being said. In everyday life, if we observe an individual who is in an emotional state, we will at first notice his facial expression, as we listen to what he says if the person is speaking (which does not necessarily imply that we attend to what he is saying). We may register the direction of his gaze, the lines of his frown, the movement of his lips, and the tone of his voice without realizing it. We also perceive other signs through his gestures and posture, registering the position of his hands, the way he sits, his foot movements and so on. All of this is mostly perceived subliminally, i.e. below the conscious level, but it informs us quite accurately about the emotional state of that person. The same thing occurs if the one "emoting" is in fact emitting no words: there may be only a very eloquent silence.

All this information constitutes a very relevant part of what globally is called "language" and is undoubtedly directly related to the emotional state of the speaker.

It often happens that someone is describing an emotional event verbally, in such a way that we immediately realize that there is an incongruity between what he is saying and what his face and gestures are expressing. "All this amuses me very much," says Mary while her face is showing unmistakable signs of distress or fear and her hands are moving nervously. Or John exclaims, "This woman really terrifies me," and says it with a very relaxed posture and an amused expression on his face. Also the tone of voice, the intonation of the sentences, all of the "how" of what is said, will indicate whether it is serious, playful or simply wrong.

All of this corroborates the fact that the semantic meaning of words is not always the most important part of a message.

**"One may lie through the mouth,"** said Nietzsche, referring to the **spoken word,** *"the accompanying gesture, however, says the truth."*

> A few days ago, I met a man socially who showed an avid interest in my work on emotions. He was a professional in his fifties, who had undergone different types of psychotherapies and also mystical experiences. At a certain point in our conversation he told me that he had gone through periods of deep depression, followed by long stretches

of therapies. He mentioned his "tachycardia" (increase in heart rate) and other physical symptoms he had when feeling "depressed." I asked him to show me how he behaved when depressed. Again he began to verbalize about his symptoms, but I insisted that what I asked him was to show me physically how he behaved when depressed. (Curiously enough this seems to be something most people have trouble with.) He began to move his hands, rapidly changing the direction of his gaze around the room; then rose from the sofa, moved restlessly around and finally sat down again.

Everything he was showing me was so typical of a very anxious person that when I asked him what emotional state he thought he was describing, he answered, somewhat surprised himself, that in fact what he was showing was what he felt when he was afraid.

This demonstrates that a cultivated, educated person, who has mastered many language subtleties and even performance techniques (he had also studied theatre), a person who had had so many experiences and therapies, can call an obvious state of anxiety, "depression."

I must say here, and will come back to it later, that for me anxiety may be considered a state of chronic fear without a clear cause and that depression may be considered sadness sustained over time.

**The frequent confusion in relation to emotional states, the 'nebulae' (cloudiness) that exist in the expressions and bodily symptoms that describe them, is due, in my opinion, to the excessive "psychologizing" through which the subject of emotion has been approached. Everything is judged by the mind, using complex analyses and interpretations. People have trouble just describing simply and clearly what happens to them when they emote.**

*"I challenge any person to try to express something without the body."* Wrote Denis Diderot around 1774 in his book *Elements of Physiology.*

It is curious to observe that when people speak about an emotional state, they usually refer to it as something abstract, impersonal and vague, as if they were describing something that happens to someone else. For example, I ask an acquaintance how she is feeling since her husband has been gone. Her response may well be vague and impersonal, "Well, you feel lonely and you don't feel like eating alone and you watch a lot of TV." Or others will say, for instance, "When I am walking in the street, I often experience a series of strange sensations, as if I were unsure," a rather interpretative and vague description, instead of referring more directly to a particular emotion, such as "my heart started pounding and I got scared." It is as if by abstracting the emotion, it ceases to exist, or would be something happening to someone else, and this is, of course, quite paradoxical.

As a consequence, this being "out of our bodies" leads to the following results: we are often completely unaware of what we are **really feeling**. Most of the time, we are daydreaming or absorbed in our thoughts, and therefore apart from the present physical moment in which we are living. In other words, **we live almost exclusively in our heads.**

> I recall a dear friend and colleague in Paris who would descend the long staircase from his apartment on his way to the University with the classical garbage bag —the requisite behavior was to leave it in the building's basement— in one hand and his attaché case containing important documents in the other. He sometimes arrived at his laboratory still carrying both bags. It is a wonder that he didn't throw the documents in the garbage pail! When I playfully made a comment on this, he told me that he used the stroll to his laboratory to "think" about his experiments.

We often say that such things happen to the "absent-minded professor." I believe that such "living in one's head" may cause people to become unbalanced.

> And where are the emotions left?

This is how I was educated. My mother wanted me to be a professional, and never taught me how to cook the delicious meals she prepared, or to knit the lovely dresses she diligently created with her own hands. As if such manual activity would diminish me, when in fact it could only have enriched and completed my education! I now recall with shame that for years, in my pride in "being an intellectual," (and thus purely "mental") I would not allow myself to "lose time" washing my clothes or preparing food! I finally woke up in my forties.

> And the emotions, where were they?

**Everything is given to us, it is in us; all the cues of what is happening are present, but we do not see them. If we just stopped for a moment and observed how we are breathing, how the muscles of our backs become tense, how we walk looking at the ground —each and all very precise signs of internal states— maybe**

we would not live with so much confusion and ignorance about our feelings; we would more easily acknowledge what happens to us and to others. We could therefore live with fewer misunderstandings and be happier. And more real.

## THE STUDY OF EMOTIONS: A PSYCHOPHYSIOLOGICAL APPROACH

Some challenges to scientific investigation of emotions are that the emotional situations that commonly occur in everyday life can rarely be elicited in laboratory conditions. In order to record physiological and expressive changes during an emotional state, complex equipment and settings are required. To provoke experimentally a genuine emotion in the laboratory is in no way an easy task, as we shall see later on.

## DEFINITION AND ANALYSIS OF AN EMOTION

> **Emotions are functional states of the entire organism that involve simultaneously physiological (organic) processes and psychological (mental) processes.**

Of this complex set of phenomena, clinical psychologists are mainly interested in the psychological processes, without much considering the underlying physiological events. Social psychologists are concerned with the communicative and expressive aspects of emotions, without relating them to particular subjective contexts. On the other hand physiologists try to study neuro-humoral or electro-physiological aspects of emotions, mainly utilizing animal subjects that obviously have no access to the subjective domain, which is exclusively human.

All these approaches to the subject rest on a dualistic view of emotional phenomena: on one side the organic processes, and on the other, the subjective aspects, as if all of them do not occur in the same brain of the same person!

This was, among others, one of the problems I had to face when I intended to continue my research on emotions at the CNRS (*Centre Nationale de la Recherche Scientifique,* French National Scientific Research Center), in my Laboratory at the *Institute of Neuroscience of the University Pierre et Marie Curie* in Paris, where I was settled at the time.

When I decided to change my research subject from pigeon vision back to my work on human emotions that I had begun in Chile, the academic members of the CNRS that annually review the scientific reports of their peers were outraged. *"Physiological research on emotions?"* They claimed. *"Emotions are a subject for poets or for clinical psychologists! Emotional behavior is very far from neuroscience, and besides it is a highly risky subject for obtaining valid experimental results."*

In those days, the late 1960's and early 1970's, and particularly in France, not only an experimental study of emotions, but also the simple word "emotion" itself, was inconceivable for scientific study. Even in the world of theatre where emotions are the core of acting, emotion was not supposed to be studied or analyzed, but just "felt."

The study of emotions has been effectively treated mostly from a purely psychological point of view. And undoubtedly what people feel in their private, subjective world is the most real and valid for them.

But one may raise the question as to whether people are truly capable of always recognizing what they feel, and if so, whether they are capable of expressing adequately what is felt.

The only possible way to have access to the internal (psychological) world of a person is through a process of introspection, that is to say, by looking into oneself. But for many years, and mainly due to the reign of behaviorism, experimental psychologists did not accept introspection as an important and in fact the only possible avenue of access into the subjective world.

Behaviorism considered human beings to be like "black boxes" from which one could only register what went in and what came out (input and output, stimulus-response).

For a long time, this point of view retarded the emergence of a more comprehensive approach to the study of emotions, since what a person feels, his thoughts, in sum, all his inner mental processes, that is to say his subjective world, can only be observed, by definition, by the person himself, and only through introspection. Then it can be communicated through language, be it verbal (spoken or written), non-verbal or by other means of which little is known but which some call reading people's auras, telepathy, extrasensory perception, and so on.

We human beings have the capacity to detect quite precisely these non-verbal signs and our judgments about them are mostly in agreement with those of other people. For example, different members of a working team will agree one morning that their boss arrived in a bad mood, even when his external behavior was apparently not different from other mornings. On what are these discrepant judgments based? Are they valid?

In the field of experimental research, is a group of observers' similar judgment valid for a scientist? Yes if they agree at a high percentage. We believe it may be totally valid provided that the observations are based on certain common rules, and the sampling is adequate and the outcome is statistically significant. For validating the expression of basic emotions, the observer's judgment is very important and represents a very interesting and essential complement to our own introspections.

Nowadays many scientists accept introspection as a valid means of access to the interior subjective world. They also acknowledge the inevitable influence of the observer upon what is observed.

In order to explore what happens physiologically during an emotion, it is necessary to enter into the "black box," and therefore the scientist needs to "slice" the emotion, so to speak, in a real or virtual manner, in order to have a "glimpse" of what is inside. In fact scientists need to open the Pandora's Box to "dis-cover" what is already there. They then have to systematize and quantify what they see, what they measure, what they alter, and express the data in formulas, recordings, graphic representations, equations, statistical tables and so on. In this way they may eventually formulate a theory or develop a model based on a well-formulated hypothesis.

But the scientist must also be open to the judgments of the observers, as I just said, and consider them as valid criteria, and especially when the object of study refers to phenomena which are so complex, and ungraspable as are emotions.

> I needed more than four years of experimental research on emotions, running completely countercurrent to the other areas of research in our laboratory in Paris, to produce clear results, ready to be published in scientific journals. Only then could we convince the CNRS (Research Council) authorities of the importance and relevance of our work.

The objective verification of precise physiological parameters and expressive behaviors typical for each basic emotion, and the development of a method for their practical application, resulted in a powerful instrument of access to the human's inner world of emotions, and the means of adequately expressing personal feelings. With such a tool available, people may learn to face personal crises and to initiate spiritual searches with more solid and concrete supports.

I believe that presently a purely cognitive approach (such as knowing the evoking stimulus) to emotional phenomena is unsatisfactory. It has been, for instance, clearly demonstrated that the impact of audiovisual messages depends much more on their emotional charge than on their rational content. This is especially clear with news on the television in which images with strong emotional meaning are those that the public remembers and comments on.

*Alba Emoting* is concerned with the expression of emotions and their strong connection to breathing patterns, without going into what situations have caused them. The focus of attention is centered on the physical and physiological aspects of emotion at the moment the emotion occurs, and to relate them to what people are feeling. It therefore is an integrated, holistic view of emotions.

## THREE LEVELS OF ACTIVATION

**I define emotion as a complex functional state of the entire organism, which includes physiological activity, expressive behavior and an inner experience, without proposing a sequential order of these three levels.**

What happens in us that cause us to say we are "moved?" A great number of physiological activities take place when we are in an emotional state. Some can be measured without invading the organism, such as heart rate, breathing, blood pressure, tear secretions, composition of the urine, or global activity of the brain neurons as measured by electroencephalography or magnetic ressonance techniques. Others have no possible, direct, noninvasive approach, such as neuro-chemical activity in the synapses (the place where neurons are connected). Still others pose ethical questions to the responsible and morally conscious experimenter, for instance placing recording electrodes in a patient's brain, or profiting from a surgery performed for other needed medical reasons.

Moreover, even those physiological parameters, which can be indirectly recorded, need complex equipment. It becomes very difficult to record what happens in the organism during spontaneous emotional outbursts. In fact there are very few scientifically confirmed data that may indicate what occurs to us organically during different emotions.

The "industry of security," to somehow give it a name, has sponsored studies whose results are not communicated to the public, and whose applications are very little known. Some examples are lie detectors and some elements recently incorporated into bank checks, which change colors according to the degree of "nervousness" of the person trying to cash a check. Also advances have been made during past years with the use of magnetic resonance imaging (MRI) to visualize brain structures that become activated during certain emotional states.

The subjective aspect of an emotion is totally personal and consequently solely accessible to the one who is feeling it –the one and only lonely observer– by what is technically called "introspection." This intimate element can only be transmitted through language, be it verbal or nonverbal.

What the observer can perceive with relative clarity are the external manifestations of the emotion the subject is feeling, which somehow allow us to say, probably without mistake, that today our boss arrived in a very sad mood, even before he has uttered a single word. We can tell it by the manner in which he walked into the office, by certain slowness in his gestures, by the expression on his face. Such expressive behavior can usually be observed with the naked eye and can be recorded directly with a camera.

But what occurs to us subjectively, again, is not sufficient to understand what an emotion is. We are many-sided creatures, organically integrated. Even if we perceive something within ourselves when we are moved, in our minds, in our thoughts, in our physiology, in our bodies, in our "feelings," we still need to be able to communicate this internal world to others. We need to learn to express our feelings when needed.

With what resources are we equipped to do this? Obviously as human beings we have verbal language. And we have, as already mentioned, other expressive means which are not linguistic: if I am happy, this mood may be reflected in my face, in my smile, in my relaxed posture, in a certain shine in my eyes. On the other hand, if I say that I feel happy, but my face has a frown, most probably the words will not convince a fine observer.

**An emotional state is therefore manifested on three parallel and interconnected levels: an expressive level (facial and postural), a physiological level (organic) and a subjective level (mental).**

And how do these three levels interact?

Though the three levels are always functionally interconnected, there is not necessarily a strict correlation among them. For instance a person may be feeling an emotion intensely (subjective mental level), accompanied by great physiological activity (organic level) and only express it slightly on the face or in the posture (expressive level). Moreover, taken to the level of behavior, which has not yet been referred to here, the action may remain totally inhibited.

> The ideal would be that people could spontaneously express what they feel with precision and clarity, as small children and people from the so-called "primitive" societies do. However, the social element is undoubtedly pertinent, and in many circumstances may become a limitation for the adequate expression of an emotion by promoting, for example, the repression of certain emotions considered to be culturally inappropriate.

The pathological extreme of dissociation among components of the three mentioned levels is the case of the "lunatic" who, when laughing says, "How sad I am." This syndrome is called in psychiatry "ideo-affective dissociation." It is certain that between a perfect coherence among all components of an emotion at one extreme, and a pathological ideo-affective dissociation on the other, there are different nuances and degrees of disassociation, as when we strongly affirm "feeling fine" while expressively revealing exactly the opposite in our faces.

Let me be more precise here in stating that I am using the terms emotional state, mood, humor, affect as essentially equivalent, since they all have, in my opinion, the same basic characteristics and include the same phenomena we refer to when we speak of emotions.

> *I am writing in my wooden house by the Chilean coast, looking through a large window that frames the lush and florid garden. It looks like a painting of nature hanging out there. The neighbors have cut some eucalyptus of a very special kind, with silvery green leaves; a tiny bird jumps from branch to branch and a white butterfly flutters its silky wings. "What is my state of mind?" I ask myself. Something between joy and melancholy, with a pinch of sadness intermingled with a certain sense of wellbeing. A moment later as a cloud is*

*passing by, I enter a tender reverie followed by a slight sensation of anxiety, as I ask myself how this book is progressing. And suddenly I feel like running off to get some lunch or to watch some TV. So there has been turmoil of fluctuating internal, mental, and emotional states in a period not longer than a couple of minutes...*

At the beginning of the 20th century, scientists who studied emotions faced the still unsolved controversy of whether *"we run because we are afraid, or we are afraid because we run."* In the first case, the action of running appears as a consequence of some internal processing: something like, *"This is dangerous, and since I cannot handle it, the best I can do in these circumstances is to run away."* In the second case, a quick and approximate estimation of the situation is made, as when we perceive something in the periphery of our visual field, which we cannot quite identify, but which gives us information that something large is approaching, so without further analysis, we run away.

This last strategy seems much more adaptive since most probably in the first case, we would have already been devoured by the lion!

We now know that certain emotional reactions are produced before the brain has had sufficient time to register the cause of that reaction. This happens because the neural circuitry involved in the emotional response (via the amygdala, the small structure located in the mid-brain) can be totally independent of the "cognitive" circuitry responsible for informing the higher brain centers (neocortex) of what has happened (via the hippocampus in the limbic system). One can therefore advance the hypothesis that the emotional response is too fast to allow a rational analysis before the actual "feeling" appears. Since there are not yet convincing scientific proofs to support this statement, it is also possible that the interpretative cognitive processing is simultaneous with the physical reactions.

We also now know that there is a remarkable interconnection both anatomical as well as functional, between the different systems that regulate our organism and that therefore, we constitute a whole that can be activated from any part. So, if I am thinking of something anxiety-producing, my back may begin to hurt, and if I have a bad cold, I may get depressed.

Nowadays we have more and more information about how the nervous system functions and more knowledge of its multiple interconnections within itself and with other systems. So we can say that our entire organism is like a big resonator and that any change, however small, in our perceptions, in our consciousness, in our thoughts, will somehow echo organically, and that bodily signals will rebound on our psyche.

The idea of a mind/body dichotomy is finally beginning to be abandoned by the great majority of scientists, particularly for those involved in the study of emotions and their relation to health. So, the brilliant ideas advanced by William James are beginning to make more and more sense.

## WILLIAM JAMES: THE JAMES-LANGE THEORY

All these years, during which I have lived with **Alba Emoting**, I have encountered unexpected well-known allies in this subject, such as Shakespeare, Garcia Lorca, Diderot, Artaud, Angeles Mastretta and others whom I will be mentioning in this book.

Far back in the shadows of my mind also lurks Charles Darwin and William James, both important names in the field of Psychology.

> One day, in around 1990, while traveling by train from Paris to London to present my work at a symposium, there suddenly and mysteriously appeared seated next to me who but William James in person! He winked at me and disappeared.
>
> As I awoke from my reverie, I found on the seat a copy of one of his articles entitled *What is an Emotion?* Which had been published in the review, *Mind*, in 1884. I began to read it right then and there and as I progressed with the reading, my attention was more and more captivated, as I felt how close his writings were to my own reflections and experiences.

I have decided to present his ideas here as they seem to me completely pertinent to the subject treated in this book.

> *(But first I will relax for a while, stretch my back and oh! one sigh... two sighs... three sighs)*

William James, a remarkable medical doctor, psychologist and philosopher, brother of the no less famous novelist, Henry James, was the first to try to describe systematically the relation existing between the subjective experience of an emotion and the concomitant body manifestations of that emotion. In 1884 he developed the theory that emotional experience is secondary to bodily changes, a proposition which had already been insinuated by Charles Darwin. Darwin had established the universality of basic emotions, mainly based on their facial and body expressions.

The theory of James is known as the *James-Lange Theory*, because the Danish physiologist, Carl Lange, independently developed the same ideas during the same period.

James stated that basic emotions –which he named "standard emotions"– were those that had a clear corporeal expression. He writes:

> *"Our natural way of thinking about these standard emotions is that the mental perception of some facts excites the mental affection called emotion, and that this latter state of mind gives rise to the bodily expression. My thesis on the contrary is that the bodily changes always follow the perception of the exciting fact, and that our feeling of the same changes as they occur is the emotion." Common sense says, we lose our fortune, are sorry and weep; we meet a bear, are frightened and run; we are insulted by a rival, are angry and strike. The hypothesis to be defended here says that this order of sequence is incorrect, that the one mental state is not immediately induced by the other, that the bodily manifestations must first be interposed between. And that the more rational statement is that we feel sorry because we cry, strike or tremble, because we are sorry, angry, or fearful, as the case may be."*

Without the bodily changes that follow the perception of an external event, our emotional life would be *"purely cognitive in form, colorless, destitute of emotional warmth."*

> *"That the heart-beats and the rhythm of breathing play a leading part in all emotions whatsoever, is a matter too notorious for proof. And what is really equally prominent, but less likely to be admitted until special attention is drawn to the fact, is the continuous co-operation of the voluntary muscles in our emotional states. Even when no change of outward attitude is produced, their inward tension alters to suit each varying mood, and is felt as a difference of tone or of strain. In depression the flexors tend to prevail, in elation or belligerent excitement the extensors take the lead. And the various permutations and combinations of which these organic activities are susceptible, make it abstractly possible that no shade of emotion, however slight, should be without a bodily reverberation as unique, when taken in its totality, as is the mental mood itself."*

We all possess the capacity to perceive the corporeality of our emotional states provided we give it the right attention. When we are worried, however slightly, we may become aware of the tensing of our eyes and our frowning; when we suddenly feel shy, something inside our throats makes us swallow, cough or clear our throats.

> *"What kind of emotion of fear would be left, if neither feelings of quickened heart-beats nor of shallow breathing, neither of trembling lips nor of weakened limbs, neither of goose-flesh nor of visceral stirrings, were present, it is quite impossible to think. Can one fancy the state of rage and picture no ebullition of it in the chest, no flushing of the face, no dilation of the nostrils, no clenching of the teeth, no impulse to vigorous action, but in their stead, limp muscles, calm breathing and a placid face?... In like manner of grief: what would it be without its tears, its sobs, its suffocation of the heart, its pang in the breast-bone?...* **I say that for us, emotion dissociated from all bodily feeling is inconceivable.**"

James postulated that if his theory were correct, it meant in his own words that:

> *"...any voluntary arousal of the so-called manifestations of a special emotion ought to give us the emotion itself."*

Our research on the Emotional Effector Patterns of Basic Emotions resulted in the Alba Emoting System which allows people, as we shall see later, **precisely to induce an emotional state by the voluntary reproduction of specific "Respiratory-Postural-Facial patterns."**

It should therefore not have surprised me that after listening to one of the first reports I gave of our findings to the scientific community at the *European Brain and Behavior Society Conference* in Jerusalem, a French colleague jumped from his seat exclaiming with quite unusual excitement for these kinds of meetings:

> *"This is the first time that I hear of an experimental demonstration of the James-Lange theory!"*

I have presented here William James' ideas in his own words —one of the few academic quotations in this book— **because the method I have developed is in fact an experimental demonstration of his theory** stated over a century ago.

[NOTE: I found this reference while reviewing the literature on the subject after we had measured and described the "Emotional Effector Patterns," and after James' mysterious apparition sitting next to me on that train going from Paris to London.]

## BASIC EMOTIONS

If we take an exploratory journey into our own emotional experience, we must agree that: **joy, sadness, anger, rage, fear, anxiety, sensuality** are states or moods through which we travel all the time in different degrees of intensity. These emotional states are so basic that if we examine ourselves attentively, we must admit that even if we do not intend to, we are perpetually oscillating among them. In fact a state of true emotional "neutrality" is very difficult to attain. We always, whether in small or large doses, somehow feel a little happy, or sad, or anxious, or friendly or in a mixture of them alternating randomly.

Sometimes these "states of mind" or "moods" present themselves in quite pure form, like primary (monochromatic) colors of the rainbow, but most frequently they mix, alternate and vary in intensity, in duration and so on. In any case they undoubtedly occupy our entire being and color almost all our perceptions so that it is quite true that "everything we look at is tinted with the color of the lenses we look through."

We may say that these "lenses" are essentially impregnated with emotional material. One morning we wake up happy because we have slept well or have had a pleasant dream, and everything looks shiny and luminous, even if the sky is overcast. But at the same time we are so labile that it only takes a minimal incident –the breakfast coffee is cold, a phone call announces something disagreeable– and our joyful mood immediately changes. So we must accept that our emotional selves are uneven, fluctuating, and permanently susceptible to react to any kind of external or internal stimuli.

Our research on the emotions started with the selection of six basic emotions. This decision right from the beginning provided a frame of reference and a delimitation of the object of study, and it speaks to the question I am always asked, "Why did we find or choose the following six basic emotions?"

I will list them again:

**Joy** (laughter, happiness)
**Sadness** (weeping, depression)
**Fear** (anxiety, terror)
**Anger** (aggression, fury)

And the two basic forms of love:

**Erotic love** (sexuality)
**Tenderness** (parental, filial love, friendship)

When we began this study in Chile, we only spoke of five basic emotions: joy, sadness, fear, anger and love. Later on, as our research progressed, it was evident that the two forms of love were subjectively, physiologically and behaviorally radically different. Very few researchers include these forms of love in their lists of basic emotions. The great majority of psychologists and investigators of this subject however agree to catalogue *joy, anger, sadness* and *fear* as basic emotions (primary or fundamental emotions as some call them).

The reasons that most of these authors give for considering them to be basic are that they all fulfill certain characteristics such as:

a) They are biologically primitive, in the sense that they have a particular evolutionary significance, in relation to the need to survive both for the individual and for the species.

b) They fill a primary need for ontogenetic development (development of the individual, independent of the species.)

c) They appear in very early post-natal development or have some elements that are already biologically programmed before birth. For example already in the second month of life, the human infant manifests behaviors that are clearly related to the first four emotions listed above, and by about 2 years is capable of naming the emotion experienced.

d) They have universal facial expressions, i.e. common to the species, and therefore are recognizable by all individuals of the same species, independent of race, gender or culture.

Our physiological recordings, as I have already mentioned, also confirmed the existence of 2 distinct breathing, postural and facial patterns for the 2 basic forms of love: one that is connected with sexuality (erotic love) and the other related to tenderness (parental love, filial love, friendship).

We therefore included these two clearly differentiated forms of *love* as basic emotions, since they have specific and universal differentiated Effector Patterns, and because both fulfill the characteristics mentioned above. One could postulate –taking the argument to the extreme– that if there were no clear and distinct universal expressive elements that help to communicate and recognize the sexual desire in another, mating would not take place and our species would become extinct. And the emotion of tenderness is essential because we would not survive without protection, especially during the first years of life.

The clear, distinct and unequivocal expression of each of these forms of love is very important to avoid misunderstandings in communicating these emotions. A gesture, a particular breath or postural attitude that is "friendly" would not be misinterpreted as "erotic."

Throughout the years of experimenting with this particular issue, I have encountered many persons, especially women, whose breathing and expressive patterns for these emotions are undifferentiated, with the consequent confusion this may cause in members of the opposite sex, leading to misunderstandings and problems.

In any case the reasons presented here as to why we consider these six emotions to be basic are not exhaustive and in no way pretend to give a full and definite academic answer to this controversial issue. Its sole purpose is to provide a general frame of reference in presenting our research, and to try at least briefly to respond to this persistent question, why do I consider these six emotions to be basic?

**A basic emotion corresponds to a physical and mental functional state of the entire organism that is different and specific for each basic emotion.**

If I am sad, I am in a total organic state that is physiologically, perceptually, experientially, expressively and intellectually different than when I am happy. **One could say that in each emotional state one almost becomes, as is expressed in Spanish, "another person" since each state embodies a different activation of the entire organism, from head to foot.**

In these different states we also perceive as different the same external reality. Coming back to the saying that "everything is seen according to the lenses through which we look," we could slightly modify it by stating, "everything is seen according to the emotional state <u>from</u> which we look."

**The basic emotions provide the essential relating code that human beings have to adjust to diverse situations without losing one's essence. It is the code that permanently "runs through" the rich and varied functioning of life, in all its complex biodiversity. They are the solid "foundation stones" for all emotions.**

As I have said before, very little is known up to now about the physiological bases that support the diversity of emotional states, or at least very few elements have been recorded and experimentally demonstrated that may differentiate one basic emotion from another.

We know, for instance, that heart rate is altered under different emotions, but such changes are non-specific, i.e. they change similarly for different emotions. Therefore an increase in heart rate by itself is not a clear indicator that would explain the subjective and expressive differences that exist between a person who is happy and one who is afraid. Neither is the amount of organic activity involved in going from deep sleep to maximally awake excitation, an indication that will tell if the excitation is of joy or of anxiety. So to emote or to be "moved" is different according to the emotion in question. To say "I am moved" does not inform whether it is with joy or with sadness. It is most probable that the physiological recordings during this vague state of "being moved" are also too global and generalized. It is also possible that it rather refers to mixed emotions or that it is all just a problem of terminology.

We were interested right from the beginning in finding some distinctive elements in the functioning of the organism that would give support to the different qualities or "colors" of the emotion one is experiencing.

> Our experimental data show that the six basic emotions become like the "corner stones" for all emotions, just as the primary colors of the rainbow are the basic fluids for the entire color spectrum.

## IS THE SUBJECTIVE EXPERIENCE OF A BASIC EMOTION THE SAME FOR EVERYONE?

If basic emotions are universally invariant, i.e. common to all humans, and if they imply the activation of the three levels mentioned above, physiological, expressive, and subjective, one could hypothesize that the same subjective feeling would correspond to the same emotion in everyone.

When John is angry, for example, could one say that his anger is subjectively similar to the anger of Paul or Mary? I propose that yes, basically it is the same, i.e. belonging to the same category, because if it were not so, then John who is feeling it, and I who am observing it, would not consistently recognize it as anger. What may certainly vary is the degree of anger both felt and expressed. So we might say that John is somewhat irritated while Paul and Mary are furious. But we identify both emotional states as belonging to the emotional category of anger.

The intensity of the emotion both in the expressive as well as in the subjective level is an important element to consider and of course will vary. If it were not so, we would not understand each other and such confusion might have dreadful consequences, because it is certainly better to walk away from people who are furious, but handle those who are just irritated with tact, trying to calm them. As we well know, different organic states are normally transmuted into different modes of action.

> "Don't we agree, Humberto Maturana, as when we danced together in our book *Biología del Emocionar y Alba Emoting, Bailando Juntos?*" (*Biology of Emotions and Alba Emoting, Dancing Together*, published with Humberto Maturana in 1996)

The internal subjective emotional state is different from person to person or from one moment to another in the same person. It is clear that the content, the cause, the degree of compromise, the intensity of the feeling, all will depend on the personal history and the particular circumstances of the emotional arousal of the individual. But, when a person is angry, that anger has a "particular color," so one can presumably name it independently of the situation that originated it. What would be strange, and terribly confusing, is that what John calls anger, Maria would call joy. I repeat that the intensity of the emotional feeling, the degree of coping with it, and the associations this anger evokes, are totally personal and circumstantial.

In fact all this is quite indemonstrable since subjective states are by definition intimate and personal, and only the one who is feeling them, has real access to their contents.

Let us accept that when I speak of basic emotions, I am referring to "pure" states, something like the monochromatic rays of light from the spectrum. So when Magdalena says that what she feels internally when she is sad is different from what Maria feels when she is sad, this is obviously impossible to demonstrate. However it is undoubtedly so, that the expressive elements and the physiological activation that both women generate must be similar, if the emotional category is the same. If it were not so, I insist, our capacities to communicate with one another would be even more complicated than they already are.

What happens is that most of the time the great majority of emotions are mixed. Paul's irritation may be contaminated, mixed or alternating with a dose of fear, while John's anger may be absolutely pure. Or Maria's sadness might be mixed with a bit of tenderness, provoking in her a sense of sweet melancholy, while what Magdalena feels and expresses is pure sadness. In such cases, we human beings have the possibility to intuitively recognize and make quite fine distinctions between "pure" and "mixed" emotional states.

**The more we are disconnected from pure basic emotions, the more complicated become our inner states, to the point that frequently we lose the capacity to identify them in ourselves and in others.**

## FROM BASIC EMOTIONS TO MIXED EMOTIONS

*Santa María, San Berenito, todo mezclado*
*Los unos mandando, los otros mandados*
*Todo mezclado…*

Saint Mary, Saint Berenito, all mixed,
Some commanding, some obeying
All mixed…

(Nicolás Guillén, Cuban poet)

My work with basic emotions has forced me to face the existence of an entire universe of expressions that, viewed from the **Alba Emoting** experience, turn out to be emotional states that are generally not labeled as such. Besides, a question always remains in the air: if there are only six basic emotions, what then are all the other emotions?

To have invaded the vast, complex and mysterious world of emotions, with a biological, physical, scientific method, which formally defines a proper and distinctive universe for each of six basic emotions, made me reformulate my approach to other human emotional expressions, and ask myself, for example, to what emotional space the following "terms" or "qualities" would belong:

```
the sublime
    the spiritual
        sensitivity
            hate
                vanity
                    illusion
                        jealousy
                            horror
                                interest
                                    indifference
                                        boredom
                                            shame
                                                modesty
                                            ambition
                                                nervousness
                                            indignation
                                        romanticism
                                    uncertainty
                                pleasure
                            ferocity
                        disgust
                    pride
                depression
pain
            ecstasy
                admiration
                    surprise
                        respect
                            guilt
                                nostalgia
                                    doubt?
```

Names for emotional states are unlimited. There is a great diversity of terms that denote sentiments, moods, behaviors or whatever name one may want to give them. Such terms could be grouped into four different categories or situations:

a) Terms that some ascribe as basic emotions and others do not, as for instance disgust and surprise.

b) Terms that may be assembled under the category of basic emotions but of longer duration, emotions that become chronic, as for instance hate (anger maintained over time), depression (chronic sadness), nervousness or anxiety (fear maintained over time).

c) Terms that we might call mixed emotions, as for instance jealousy, pride, shame, ambition, nostalgia.

d) Terms that undoubtedly imply higher (sublime) emotions, that are learned and which require a certain maturity, such as respect, admiration, ecstasy, spirituality, devotion, and so on.

Since the discovery of the Emotional Effector Patterns of the basic emotions, the practical application of **Alba Emoting** has convinced me even more that words such as sentiment, mood, and temperament, all refer to emotional states that are only distinguished by different degrees in duration, intensity or proportion of mixtures of basic emotions. In fact most human behavior has at its root, an emotional state.

## INTENSITY AND DURATION OF AN EMOTIONAL STATE

In relation to concepts that imply "emotionality," **Alba Emoting** establishes distinctions with respect to temporality (duration), intensity, and degree of mixture of basic emotions.

In the scientific literature on the subject of emotions, most authors call emotions only those episodes that are very short, lasting a few seconds or minutes. In this sense emotions are only considered as brief episodic reactions to a stimulus, which reach a maximum and then decline. If the emotional phenomenon lasts longer, it would not be an emotion but rather a "mood."

The position I take here is that emotions may be "phasic" if they are short-lived or "tonic" if they are maintained in time. For example, to cry at painful news would be a "phasic" emotional reaction, while to be sad about the same painful news for many days —or weeks, months or years— would be the same emotion but transformed into an "tonic" or chronic state. People in such circumstances will say that they are depressed or in a sad mood. So they will call emotion what I call "phasic emotion," and mood, what I call "tonic emotion."

It is important to understand this distinction with precision. **Alba Emoting**, with its formal structure, organizes the terms and concepts that are normally used to describe different emotional states. So to be in a bad temper is to be irritated for a long time; to wake up in a bad mood, is to be angry; to "feel happy" is to be in the emotional state of joy; "to be depressed" reflects a state of sadness maintained over time, and to be anxious is basically to have lasting fear. This does not mean that the emotion is present evenly all the time; rather it appears in waves, coloring the person's general mood, providing an emotional tonality that will impregnate his/her entire behavior.

Basic emotions are generally "phasic" reactions, that is to say transient responses that are directly related to "emotogenic" situations, i.e. situations generating those emotions. These responses are usually translated into actions: laughing, weeping, attacking, running away, caressing, flirting, making love, etc.

But basic emotions can also be transformed into "tonic" emotions, i.e. become chronic emotional states sustained a long time. These I call "moods." To be afraid in a dangerous situation is a totally adaptive emotional "phasic" reaction, but to live terrorized by that memory for a long time, though while in the same emotional category of fear, becomes transformed into a non-adaptive "tonic" state of anxiety.

In the phenomenon we call mood, the specific stimulus or situation that triggered the corresponding emotion is not present anymore, so the maintained emotional state becomes very un-adaptive and may easily be transformed into neurotic behavior. In this way we may become nervous or anxious for many days in anticipation of a situation that worries us, and that we have to face. If someone asks us what is wrong, we will rarely admit that we are afraid, probably because we do not realize what is bothering us. However during those days we go around with all the typical symptoms of anxiety: we have a stomach ache, we sleep badly, and we have trouble concentrating.

In my own experience, paying attention to the organic manifestations of my moods, I can more easily discover the basic emotion that is underlying my behavior. In the above example, if we paid attention to the person's breathing, we would most probably have recognized the presence of fear.

So "moods" are intermingled basic emotions presented diffusely, fluctuating over time, but always keeping a characteristic emotional "tone" that differentiates them from other emotional states or other "moods."

With this postulate in mind we can consider that anxiety is basically a chronic state of fear, and depression a chronic state of sadness, since the great majority of the components comprising those corresponding "Effector Patterns" are always present in each.

Another element that contributes to the variability of different emotional states is related to the intensity dimension. It is curious that even though the intensity of an emotional action is one of its most relevant features, psychologists have given so little attention to it in the majority of empirical studies that have been done.

Very little is known, for instance about the relation between the emotional intensity a person is feeling and the different concomitant physiological and behavioral parameters. Most probably such a relationship is not very precise and definitely non-linear, so that the internal emotional experience and the external behavioral manifestation may, to a certain extent, vary independently as I have said before. So someone may be furious and only exteriorize a slight (though eloquent) expression of that anger.

But as we have seen the observer may still recognize the emotional category even with such a small external manifestation. However he will probably not capture the intensity of anger the person is feeling. On the other hand it is possible that someone expresses a great fear very intensely, just for the purpose of manipulating others. This is often seen in children's games, such as "the monster is coming." (One should be careful with such games since children do not always distinguish "theatricality" from reality.)

In my experience, a basic emotion maintained over time is generally transformed into a mixed or blended emotion. Precisely because it lasts longer, it necessarily becomes impregnated with mental activity (psychological interpretations, and value judgments, among others).

In order to understand emotional behaviors lasting through time, one has to differentiate biological-psychological time from chronological time. We cannot forget that chronological time is a human invention rising from the human mental domain and not from the human emotional biological realm.

If for instance we analyzed why a small healthy child does not have "tonic" emotions, we could say that it is so because the child's psychological time coincides with his biological time. Basic emotions therefore would essentially enter into the category of phasic emotions, since they are basically related to biological time.

Tonic emotions, on the other hand, are natural soil for the expression of mixed emotions. However, mixed emotions may also be phasic (acute and of very short duration). Who has not experienced or seen someone crying from anger or having an abrupt attack of jealousy (typical mixed emotion) that may fade out in a few seconds?

## MIXED EMOTIONS

In fact, another of the problems for the study of emotions is the vast terminology that tries to cover the infinite moods that invade us once we enter into the complex psychological, historical, and cultural setting of our adult universe.

When emotions are transformed into such chronic emotional states, they generally are presented and felt as a mixture of basic emotions, tinted with psychological interpretations. For instance, when a small child is angry his anger is not mixed with say fear, and when he laughs it is like a crystal clear waterfall of joy. But as we leave childhood those basic emotions that were so natural and fluid begin to get mixed, losing their "purity," their "mono-chromaticity."

We adults rarely function with pure basic emotion.

However, a mixed emotion, even impregnated with psychological interpretation, always has a basic organic structural component that corresponds to the "Effector Patterns" of the combined basic emotions involved seen from the non-cultural and non-psychological Darwinian approach I am taking here.

> **The basic emotion is the skeleton that supports any more complex emotional state. From the moment we accept that by definition every emotional state is linked to the body, it is possible to discover the underlying basic emotions which are present in any emotional state, by starting from the "Effector Patterns" Alba Emoting distinguishes, and from there enter into the subjective emotional space.**
>
> **For Alba Emoting, Emotions ARE the encounter between the Psyche and the Body.**

From this point of view, it is possible to analyze any mixed emotional behavior, decomposing it into its "basic" components.

Let us explore the case of a leader. A leader needs to be firm, decisive, daring and charismatic. According to our method, such traits of character require a good dose of anger, which corresponds to a basic emotion that predisposes a person to go forwards, to attack.

But a leader also needs optimism and faith, so a dose of joy is needed. A leader must also possess a spirit of solidarity, which requires tenderness and care, and finally, a small dose of seduction is important, so a grain of sexuality would complete the mixture.

The combination of these basic emotional patterns, in different proportions, gives a kind of recipe for understanding, developing and building the behavior that a leader requires. Such combinations also help to modulate a typical mixed emotion, for instance jealousy, which corresponds to a mixture of anger, fear, sadness and a pinch of sexuality.

There are authors who call basic emotions, primary emotions, especially because of the prominence of biological processes, and consider other emotions as secondary, learned during the process of socialization. But many have begun to accept that such secondary emotions get their "emotional tone" because of their connection to basic emotions. If this is viewed from the standpoint of **Alba Emoting** we could say, for example, that gratitude could be based on the primary emotion of joy, while the sense of guilt could be annexed to the primary emotion of fear.

The open challenge then is to study more systematically these different emotional states, finding the right proportion of different blends, through their physical, postural expressions, and more importantly, through their breathing characteristics.

Just as on a painter's palette, where mixing two primary colors produces a third one, the mixture of two basic emotions results in a new (mixed) emotion. In this way, for instance, pride would be a mixture of joy and anger; melancholy a mixture of sadness and tenderness, and so on.

Summing up, our study considers basic emotions to be the fundamental structures from which mixed emotions are organized. These mixed emotions correspond to the great majority of emotions present within the vast spectrum of human emotional behavior.

### No hay cosa como callar

*Toda melancolía*
*nace sin ocasión,*
*y así es la mía*
*que aquesta distinción*
*naturaleza di– a la melancolía y a la tristeza.*

All melancholy
is born without occasion,
and so is mine
that such a distinction
nature makes between melancholy and sadness

(In *"There's Nothing Like Keeping Silent"* by Calderon de la Barca)

Generally we adults live our daily lives, with mixed emotions. When people begin to learn to get consciously in contact with their basic emotions, in their most unadulterated (pure) forms, through **Alba Emoting**, they are very surprised.

I remember that at a workshop I conducted for a group of young psychologists, one of the participants started to reproduce, following my instructions, the Effector Pattern of anger for a couple of minutes. He told me after finishing the exercise that it was the first time in his life that he could clearly feel anger without the sensation of disgust and the wish to vomit that he usually had when he began to get angry. Talking later about his personal life, he told us that as a child his mother always scolded him when he had an outburst of anger, and that he then reacted with a need to vomit.

What I want to highlight here is that the mere conscious reproduction of the Effector Pattern of anger allowed this young man to have a direct access to that emotion in its most pure form, bypassing the mixture in which it had been submerged. It was not necessary to go through a long psychological interpretation of his childhood trauma.

Let us see how these mixed emotions present themselves when one begins to work with the method. One can easily see in the learning process how emotions are mixed in the untrained person. Here are some comments I made to a person who was trying to reproduce a breathing pattern for the first time.

> *There was a moment when a certain sadness began to infiltrate while you were trying to follow my instructions for the laughing pattern. There is such richness in all the body and face muscles, that if some of what I call "parasite movements (I say parasite, because they do not belong to the instructed pattern, in the case of the example here, laughter) begin to intermingle unintentionally, then the emotional arousal of joy cannot appear. The pattern is so precise that if one part of it is not there or you begin to execute a slightly different breathing to the one indicated, the emotion corresponding to the instructed pattern cannot appear, and so another emotional state emerges.*

A good metaphor for this could be that the Effector Pattern of an emotion is like a key that only opens one door. With practice in the method, it is possible to "decontaminate" the true basic emotion from the ones which I call "parasites" and which we start collecting as we go along in our lives.

There are undoubtedly powerful psychotherapeutic implications and numerable applications of this proposed method that are now being explored.

> *I have a little key*
> *For whoever wants to use it.*
> *He who sees it,*
> *Feels it,*
> *Expresses it,*
> *Cannot forget it…*
>
>     *Go, go and find it*

## II. EXPERIENTIAL REPORTS

> *Acuérdate señor mío,*
> *de tus nobles juramentos;*
> *y lo que juró la boca*
> *no lo desmientan tus hechos.*
>
> Remember, my lord,
> Your noble oaths;
> And let not what the mouth swore
> Be denied by your actions.
>
> (Sister Juana Inez de la Cruz)

With the purpose of rapidly immersing the reader in the spirit and practice of ***Alba Emoting***, I will now present some first-hand personal reports of what has happened to people who have worked directly with me, at different levels of learning and experience.

> *"We were in Paris, in your apartment on the twentieth floor, when you were just starting to apply the Alba Emoting method—which at that time wasn't called that. Without giving me any instructions whatsoever, you asked me to express anger and to express fear. To do this, I turned back to a moment when I felt fear, when I saw a trolley bus run over a woman and saw blood, something that has always scared me. You asked me to express that fear and I did so.*
>
> *Later, we found another situation in which I had felt rage. I remembered fighting with some friends and I acted out how I felt that anger. Immediately after, you taught me how to express the emotional pattern of anger and then of fear, giving me the corresponding instructions. As soon as I did this, in a second, all my existential anguish disappeared.*

*What happened? First of all, I realized that in the human being, in me, there was an underlying core of dissatisfaction; I wasn't aware of what it was, but at that moment, while executing those physical patterns, that dissatisfaction acquired another dimension. And what was that dimension?* **That inside me was anger that I didn't know how to express. I expressed it badly and, quite the opposite, I expressed it as fear.**

*Well, it was earth-shaking, because such an experience structures you. In a second I became a coherent being who expresses what he feels: I feel rage, I express it and therefore I am an ethical, moral, an honest man; I am a man who, when he says something, does it, and when I do something, I say it; and I understand it from within. Finally, everything fell in place.*

*At that moment, I felt myself living the whole dimension of empathy that one has with heroes of literature, Sandokan, Hamlet, all that. Therefore, performing an emotional pattern with the* **Alba Emoting** *method is, for me, living in a second the real authentic dimension of being, in a world where it is impossible to learn to express that being. It's the breathing, which in a second carries you into something perfect, strong... It cleanses you and also enables you to understand other existing processes such as mixed emotions and the states of the soul.*

*So, when I breathed the emotional pattern of rage, I was expressing that state which is anger and which I had always expressed badly and that therefore was not worth expressing because it frustrated me. Now, in a second, life took on different colors, a different luminosity. Even the ugly colors, sad colors like grey and dead sounds became vivid, everything worked and fit in perfectly with the here and now, with the tragic sense of living, with the saga; everything took on a meaning. I'm telling you all this in the language of the present. Perhaps I couldn't have expressed it at the time, but basically, this is it."*

This is the report of PS, one of my first "experimental subjects" in the application of the **Alba Emoting** method. He wrote it twenty-five years after his experience with the method, and always tells it to whoever wants to listen. According to him, it changed his life. I have transcribed it here with all the strength and the passion of his account, without changing a single syllable.

Another testimony comes from a basic **Alba Emoting** workshop, which I directed not long ago, for a weekend, in Santiago. After it was over, I invited the participants to come to my home a week later, so that we could all share what they had experienced during the week.

One of the participants, a dentist who was married and had two children, arrived that day unexpectedly accompanied by his wife who had not attended the workshop. He called me aside to ask if she could stay for the meeting, as it seemed important for her to share in what he had experienced. He perceived that she was often very anguished and thought that sharing with the group, what he had experienced during the workshop, might help her. When it was his turn to talk about what he had experienced during the week, he said the following words, which again I have transcribed word for word:

> *I don't know what's wrong with her (referring to his wife)… she has problems at work, she suddenly goes around as if she were annoyed, I perceived something… And the day before yesterday, when she fell asleep beside me, she started to breathe like this (he demonstrates the breathing pattern for fear that he learned at the workshop) … and I started to remember that she had also breathed like that the previous nights. Sometimes at night, I would wake up and could hear that she complained in sighs, saying ah, ah, ah, and I imagined that she had problems, like everyone else, which she deals with quite well. This worried me, but now it really alarms me because I feel that she's in a terrible state of anxiety, which I can recognize as such after attending your workshop. This is the experience that caused the most impact on me this week, that is, realizing exactly what she was experiencing I would love to transmit my experience with Alba Emoting to her, but I don't know how… that's why I brought her here."*

After this account, which I recorded with the due permission of all the participants, I turned to the wife who was sitting beside her husband, wringing her hands and breathing rapidly, and invited her to participate. With a broken but clear voice, she said the following:

> *What I feel has been coming on for some time but I haven't acknowledged it and the truth is that I'm in pretty bad shape, or…let's say…; well, the positive thing about all of this is that now I've become aware that I've got to do something about it, I think… I never believed I had reached this state of anguish and it shook me, because I realized it when he came back from the course (referring to her husband upon his return from the workshop)… I'm a person who is totally unlike most of the people who are here, or better said… I'm unimaginative, totally dedicated to the office, to finances, to money and*

*whatever, all of which are stressful and which… I have managed all my life… I refuse to admit that these things can't be solved through the mind; I reject medication, I reject psychologists, I'm a super girl and I… I'm in control, and now for the first time I have to admit that I'm not. So, when he said he was coming to this course…, I didn't take much notice and told myself that this was a psychology course or something like it. When he returned on Sunday, he was quite enthusiastic, wanting to go deeper into this kind of thing and he spoke to me with so much enthusiasm…. But the truth is that I was in such a state of anxiety, so tense, so resentful, that I didn't listen to a thing… until, well, the thing blew up in terms of my anguish and my depression, and then he said let's go to this meeting so that you can listen and then take the course, which I think will be good for you.…*

After she had finished her account, which I have transcribed, I led her through an exercise using the breathing pattern for sadness without explaining where this kind of breathing would lead her. After a short while the woman started to cry her heart out. I let her weep, instructing her to continue with the corresponding breathing pattern. After a while –no more than three minutes–, we led her through a very complete "Step-Out" (the technique used to exit from an emotion, which is described later), and then spoke of other things, while we had tea. Two weeks later, I phoned her to ask her how she was. She told me that she felt better, felt less choked up and that talking with her husband, she had noticed that she was more relaxed and sleeping better. I asked her what had happened when she was doing the breathing exercise that led her to tears that day, and she answered the following:

*"The instructions which you were giving me about the breathing pattern were easy to follow, **because it is something physical** (my own emphasis). On the other hand, to imagine, to identify sensations, to describe through imagination what one is feeling is much harder because it is more concealed."*

She added that, in fact, after crying and then changing her breathing back to a normal rhythm, she felt more serene, which was usually quite difficult for her.

I mention this particular testimony because it is a good example of one of the many results that I have observed over years of applying the **Alba Emoting** method with different people. Immediately after executing the emotional patterns, almost to their surprise, people generally become rapidly and clearly conscious of their own emotions, and learn to express them truly. Then, with more practice, they acquire the ability to recognize emotions in others more accurately.

The case described above is that of a couple who have been together for over twenty years, where the husband has recognized the emotional state of his wife by the way she breathed at night, which he had learned to recognize as anxiety (which is none other than fear).

While I transcribe these notes, I leave the account of these testimonies aside for a while because I remember that in a few hours' time, I have a doctor's appointment, which is very important to me. I feel nervous. I'm scared.

Then I stop writing and I do an exercise using my own method:

*I stand with my back straight, feet parallel, in line with the outer limits of my hips; I fix my gaze on a dot on the far horizon, with open eyes and relaxed facial muscles. In this position, without forcing it, I breathe quietly, softly and relaxed, maintaining an even rhythm of breathing in and breathing out. I synchronize the breathing rhythm with an arm movement, taking my clasped hands over my head in a "wide arch" until they reach the back of my neck, while breathing in through my nose. Then I exhale through my lips as if I were softly blowing out an invisible candle, while simultaneously I return my arms to their initial position, keeping my hands lightly clasped until they rest slightly below my pubis. I consciously repeat the same sequence at least three times.*

*Three deep breaths,*
*Air entering through the nose,*
*Softly leaving through the mouth....*

And I have become calm. I have achieved this through these simple physical actions, which are very precise and far more efficient in changing my emotional state than the mental order to calm down.

**This procedure which I have called "Step-Out," and which literally means "to exit," constitutes one of the essential elements of the Alba Emoting method.**

In Santiago, a businesswoman shares her experience immediately after doing the exercise described above to exit from an emotion.

*"I entered deeply into my sadness and cried it all out. However, I did not lose control and felt secure using the "Step-Out" to exit the emotion. This did not happen before, as it always takes several hours for me to come out of a sad mood."*

After an argument, Alicia, a domestic helper, continued crying desperately. She had accumulated a lot of sadness. I taught her how to execute the breathing for sadness over her own tears for a few minutes, followed by a good Step-Out. Then I taught her the breathing pattern for laughter. A few days later I learned, in her own words, what she had felt:

*"I was crying and couldn't stop. I felt fine when you led me through the breathing that taught me how to cry and then to laugh and then suddenly I stopped crying. I felt serene, relaxed and all that. Since then, my nervous state has disappeared; I feel fine, relaxed."*

All these examples illustrate one of the first effects that immediately appear in the person who executes the specific breathing pattern for a basic emotion: the person "enters," to use an expression, into the corresponding emotion, as a consequence of the exercise. The emotion is provoked by an external situation or a memory, and this is surprising to him/her. At the same time, the carrying out of another breathing exercise, enables him/her to immediately exit from the induced emotional state (the Step-Out described above), without remaining "stuck," so to speak, in the emotion.

**It is important to note that the whole process occurs in a state of lucidity, by carrying out the simple and precise physical actions indicated.**

Another report: Francisco, a business consultant, an intelligent and refined forty-five year-old man, had trouble expressing anger.

His creativity and ability to innovate paled beside his difficulty to express himself firmly and decidedly when necessary. Thus, he was never able to demand that his fees be paid on time; he tended to ask for things too benevolently and often became depressed, falling into what he himself termed as a state of "self-pity" (the "poor me" syndrome). At the workshop in which he participated, we led him through an exercise which had been developed along the lines of the anger pattern. A few weeks later, he sent me a letter. I have transcribed the most pertinent paragraphs below:

*During the workshop, I was able to realize that my greatest difficulty lay in expressing the feeling of anger, and that I have lost many of the things I could have got from life, by not knowing how to express it at the right moment, and substituting self-pity for it. However some of the personal experiences I have had after the workshop have shown me that it is something that can be corrected.*

*Some days ago I was finishing an article that I wanted to publish in the Sunday edition of the El Mercurio (a Chilean daily newspaper). However, I thought that the possibility of an unknown author having a first article published on a Sunday was very remote. I then decided to put into practice what I had learned at the* **Alba Emoting** *workshop. I did the breathing exercises and adopted the body stance for the feeling of anger. In this condition, I wrote a letter to the editor offering my article for publication in the following Sunday edition. After finishing the letter, I put the "Step-Out" into practice and was able to clearly feel the change in the sensation I was experiencing. A few days later, I repeated the same exercises and phoned the editor, who asked me to send him the article so that he could read it. The next day he called me to say that even though it was much longer than normal, it would be published in its entirety, without omissions, in the following Sunday paper."*

In his letter, Francisco then describes a dream he had around that time and which he attributes to the power of the method. He saw himself looking in a mirror in his father's house, but the face he saw belonged to someone else. Then, in his dream, facing the mirror he placed all his energy and rage in an angry scream, after which his own image immediately appeared clearly reflected. And he adds:

*"When I woke up, I understood the dream's message: I have spent half of my life looking at myself in my father's mirror and, of course, the image which that mirror reflects isn't my own, but the one that my father wants me to be. When I allowed myself to express the feeling of anger, which I, myself, had constantly inhibited, my real image then appeared in the mirror and I recovered my peace of mind."*

He then ends the letter remembering the day when his father gave him his first wristwatch (he was eleven years old) on the condition that he would learn not to lose his temper.

*"Since that day, to deserve the watch —and the love of my parents—, I inhibited any show of rage, to such a point that I became divorced after twenty years of marriage, without ever having shown anger to my former wife and without having raised my voice to her even once. Every time a feeling of rage surfaced, a few seconds later self-pity, or some other psychological mechanism, turned it into sadness."*

Anne-Lise Gabold, a distinguished, award-winning Danish actress, whom I have worked with using the method on several occasions, both in group seminars and in private sessions, advising her, among other activities, to work on the emotional analysis of scripts which she was preparing for several of her roles, writes to me:

*"Working with the **Alba Emoting** method, after all the techniques I have learned and used throughout my life as a professional actress, I feel a renewed emotional vitality in my acting. The more I use **Alba Emoting**, the more I realize the psychologically unhealthy amount of effort and tension I had to use to produce emotions. With **Alba Emoting** I can now enter more deeply into the emotion, with the safety valve of being able to exit at will, without getting caught up in it. This gives me great liberty."*

Simona, a thirty-five year old Neapolitan actress, a year after attending an international seminar that I offered on the method in southern France, wrote to me this note:

*"Preparing for an audition in Montreal, I had to play a long scene laughing, when Zerbinette meets Geronde (in Moliere's Les Fourberies de Scapin) before an important theatre director. I was terrified of not being able to laugh at will. So I remembered the pattern for laughter, which I learned during your workshop in France and, even though it was difficult at first, I was able to sustain incredible peals of laughter over a long period on the day of the audition. I wanted to send you an enormous MERCI.*

Vicky, a craftswoman and housewife, who has been in contact with the method at different times, tells me the following:

*"I have been in psychotherapy for many years, both in Chile and abroad, and I feel that if we'd used Alba Emoting, I would have been able to recognize and discard far more quickly, many of the layers of protection that I have used for so long. Now that I am familiar with this method, I am able to distinguish far*

*better what emotional state I'm in, and am less frightened of simply feeling. Besides, I can now ask myself why I feel some emotion or another, and learn to choose the best course of action. The "Step-Out" often helps to calm me down and lower the level of anxiety."*

As I have said before, I have noted down these testimonies exactly as they happened over different periods and in different places, in order to rapidly introduce the reader in what occurs to people of different backgrounds, experiences and interests when they use the ***Alba Emoting*** method.

# III. PUBLISH OR PERISH

Although testimonies such as those presented in the previous chapter are a good complement to the experimental findings of our work, in the scientific community it is essential to publish them in peer-reviewed scientific journals. The unquestioned slogan is "publish or perish."

Therefore, once experiments have ended and the results analyzed, it is necessary to describe them in detail, in precise language, place them in a theoretical frame of reference, relate them to data published by other authors, compare the conclusions obtained with the original hypothesis and finally project them into future perspectives and developments. In the way experimental work progresses, it often occurs that the direction it takes may not necessarily follow the original hypothesis. It is a well-known fact that great discoveries often arise from the collateral arabesques that experimental results may make.

Once the experiments have ended and the results have been analyzed, a first draft is written. However, a long time may pass before the article itself is finally published. Besides the multiple versions written by the author or, more frequently, by the authors and collaborators who participated on the research team during the different phases or aspects of the experience (something like the associates of a business enterprise) and, after applying the well-known self-censures, corrections and interpretations, the manuscript is finally sent in triplicate, in a precise format that is rigorously adjusted to the requirements of the specialized journal to which the article is submitted, to be judged and determined whether it is adequate for eventual publication.

The adventure (as with any true undertaking, any true enterprise) does not end there. As a first step in the procedure and in a lapse of time that will depend on the fluctuations of the editors' timing and/or postal delays, the main author may receive a card that indicates that the manuscript has arrived safely. With this receipt the author knows at least that the journal in question considers the manuscript to be thematically valid.

However, all this is only the beginning of another long and systematic process in which anonymous colleagues, that are specialists in the research subject and are part of the journal's editorial board or ad hoc consultants, review the manuscript. This stage of the procedure is long, usually taking 3 to 6 months, ending in the full acceptance of the paper –which rarely occurs– or in a conditional acceptance which requires changes in the presentation of results or in the style of writing, (which often means that the manuscript has to be entirely rewritten), or in total refusal. Such refusal may be due to the fact that the editor-consultant considered the work to be unoriginal, to have serious methodological errors, or that the experimental data were insufficient and/or not statistically valid.

Throughout my life as a scientist I have published a great number of articles on the psychophysiology of emotions and on other subjects relating to neuroscience, such as the mechanism of visual perception in pigeons, the role of cerebral structures in animal learning and the physiological mechanisms of attention in the monkey, among others. One of the published articles in 1991 on the subject of emotions is reproduced in full at the end of this book (See Appendix I).

## LEAVING CHILE ACROSS THE ANDES

In October 1973, I left while still in Chile with very few belongings, among which were some drafts of our initial results. They did not contain the Emotional Effector Patterns or refer to **Alba Emoting** as such, but contained rudimentary aspects and our initial research on the subject of basic emotions.

> I remember having written up our first results in English while still in Chili in order to have them published abroad. I departed for New York full of enthusiasm, with a draft version of the manuscript under my arm, to meet with the chief editor of one of the most prestigious theatre journals of the United States. It was certainly quite unusual for a person from the scientific world to try to publish physiological, experimental data in a theatre journal. However, it referred to original work that could be applied to the work of actors. For

almost an hour, the editor listened attentively to my vivid and passionate description of our discoveries. I remember very well that as he sat on a sofa listening in silence, he kept stroking his black cat. With hardly a comment, he asked me to send him the full manuscript as soon as possible, which I did when I returned to Chile.

Contrary to what normally occurs in scientific journal submissions, as I have already mentioned, i.e. the editors send a receipt for the original manuscript, and later a letter of acceptance, with or without objections, or a refusal, my shipment was followed by no response whatsoever. A year later I got a letter from a professor of a Theatre School of an American University in which he mentioned having heard from an actor about a very interesting training method that we had developed in Chile. I answered, expressing my surprise as to how he had obtained such information from still-unpublished experimental work. I remember that I even asked him for advice as to what to do when an editor does not acknowledge a shipment or return a manuscript. He advised me to resend it to the, by then, new editor. I did so, and once again I came up against the same frustrating silence and no response.

Since it was very important for us to communicate our preliminary results in print, in order to establish priority over our discovery in the event someone took the ideas and had them published before we did (these are rules of the scientific community), we rewrote our work in Spanish and had it published in a very good Chilean inter-disciplinary journal of *Science and Technology* (*Orbita*, 9:8-20, 1972), that unfortunately has been discontinued.

In addition, right after the military coup d'état in 1973, we published a second article in collaboration with Guy Santibáñez, with the physiological recordings, entitled, *"Training Emotional Effection in Humans: Significance of its Feedback on Subjectivity."*

As I write, I recall that we mentioned the word "humans" in the title, because the article was to appear in the *Annals of a Latin-American Symposium* called *The Psychobiology of Learning* that we organized in Santiago, where the great majority of contributions were animal studies. To be more clear, in the same volume I am co-author with other colleagues of a research study on cardiac activity during a learning test in the Lobster (yes, the lobster, the same one that one eats), and another article on "Color Vision in Pigeons".

With the two publications of our first experiments on emotional patterns under my arm, I left Chile, crossing the Andes without joy in my heart.

## IN PARIS, BY THE SEINE RIVER

After stopping in Buenos Aires and traveling through the Iguaçu Falls, I landed in Sao Paulo, Brazil where we stayed for almost a year with my Chilean friend and colleague Carlos Martinoya at the Department of Experimental Psychology of the Universidade de Sao Paulo working on a research project on Color Vision in the Ant.

After publishing a couple of articles on that subject, we went to Paris. There I immediately got a position at the CNRS (French National Scientific Research Center), and continued my scientific activities at the Laboratory of Psychophysiology at the University of Pierre et Marie Curie.

Unfortunately there I had to set aside the subject of basic emotions for a long time. In fact, to my great regret, it was recommended to me to leave my work with human emotions out of my *curriculum vitae*, because at the time it was not well thought of for an expert in Pigeon vision (that was me) to also be interested in scientifically exploring the world of human emotions....

It was then that I decided to use my spare time for working with the Emotional Patterns in Denmark, with a group of young actors from the Rimfaxe Theatre and later with the *Teaterklanen*, both directed by the Chilean theatre director, Horacio Muñoz, great friend of mine who was established in Copenhagen. There we jointly created the *Center for Theatre Investigation*.

It was during those very creative Danish weekends and vacation periods that the original ideas and findings we had started in Chile were developed, especially in what concerned their direct application to the work of actors.

The French have a very good expression to reflect perseverance in pursuing what we believe in. They say that it is to "avoir la suite dans les idées," which literally means to have continuity in one's ideas.

Back in Paris, I recovered my academic thematic thread with emotions and, putting together the Chilean and the Danish experiences, I wrote an article entitled *Emotional Effector Patterns: a Psycho-physiological Method for training Actors*, and sent it to the interdisciplinary *Journal of Social and Biological Structures*. Once again, it was a long editorial odyssey. It was the first article to present extensively our research applied to the work of actors. We were certainly intruding on alien domains, and were faced with specialization and territoriality, unassailable castles where only initiated specialists cross the drawbridge. However, I thought that since this journal was interdisciplinary, as is clear from its name, it was probably the appropriate place to publish our article.

> The manuscript reached the hands of a theatre expert. After about three months, I remember receiving three sheets of closely written comments, including an angry diatribe against us, daring scientists, who had the boldness (in fact he used the word "chutzpa," a colloquial American word taken from "Yiddish," a German-Jewish dialect) to carry out experiments from which a method emerged that was useful for actors! However, in spite of his editorial indignation, he recognized the originality of our contribution and stated that provided certain changes were made in the presentation and certain doubts cleared, he would recommend it for publication.
>
> Again, a few months elapsed in re-writing, reformulating, reordering and clarifying some unclear sections, all of which is the positive side to editorial comments. Finally a very much-improved version was submitted.

*All's well that ends well*

The happy ending also had an unexpected epilogue. A few months after the article had been published, the editor again wrote to me saying that since he really considered our work to be very original, he wanted to ask some international academic personalities from different specialties to comment on our research. So a year later, about ten of these comments were published, followed by my rejoinder.

Concluding this story, I must say that this particular publication with all its echoes has been very instrumental in helping our work to become known. It has opened doors and contacts with colleagues from many countries, some of whom have come to work with me or have invited me to conferences. In addition, a few students of theatre, anthropology and psychology have written their doctoral theses on the subject.

Finally, some years later, the complete article appeared, together with a selection of important contributions to the theatre, in a book edited by Phillip Zarilli, a specialist in oriental drama, entitled *Acting (re)-considered*.

## MEASURING RESPIRATORY RHYTHMS

The time had come to create a laboratory in Paris to continue my research on the psychophysiology of emotions. Until then, as I have already said, my research group was part of the Laboratory of Sensory Psychophysiology at the University of Pierre and Marie Curie, in Paris where we had arrived after crossing the Atlantic from Brazil.

Our line of research with Carlos Martinoya and our subsequent publications had been centered on the study of visual perception in pigeons. We measured the bird's visual acuity, depth perception, form, and color discrimination. In short, we explored how pigeons see the world. Students, conferences, publications and annual reports to the CNRS (French National Scientific Research Council) I belonged to, were centered on those subjects. Until then, my escapades to emotions and actors were still strictly extra-curricular activities, and in Denmark. However, the experiences we had initiated in Chile needed to be replicated in a larger number of subjects, in order to systematize, develop, and validate our findings.

As our Parisian laboratory did not provide the required space or conditions for such a study, I slowly and patiently started to equip a space that would be adequate for research on humans and not on pigeons, a totally different ecosystem! My French colleague, Madeleine Lemeignan, who was on our pigeon team, also agreed enthusiastically with the change of subject. So we outfitted our laboratory with rugs and couches to make it more attractive, and I invited the actors I had worked with on the Effector Patterns in Denmark to come.

> I recall the turmoil produced by the presence of these blond, Nordic youngsters, with their arty clothes and a style more appropriate for the acting world than for the world of austere Science, wandering through the cold corridors.

So with them as experimental subjects, we began to make systematic recordings of their breathing patterns and other physiological variables.

A scientific discovery can come about very quickly as an intuitive glimpse or as a product of chance. However, in order to be accepted and scientifically convincing, it needs to be followed by the systematic confirmation of what has been found, and this can take years. So first comes the tentative exploration of the new territory, often based on a hypothesis or intuition, and then the discovery emerges –if it emerges at all, as there are many tentative approaches that lead nowhere–, then come the confirmation, systematization, publication and finally the application.

I have had the privilege to take the lead in all these stages. When the experiences, analysis of the results and their interpretation had concluded, preparation for publication started again. Once more, another kind of specialists had to be faced; this time it was experts in respiration. Why didn't we measure oxygen consumption? And what happened to carbon dioxide during exhalation?

The article was worked on over and over again, objections cleared and finally it was published as "Specific Respiratory Patterns Distinguish between Basic Emotions" in the *International Journal of Psychophysiology*. As I have mentioned elsewhere, the full text of this article has been included in Appendice I.

This article was essential for establishing the scientific credibility of the method, and it is quoted whenever the subject of breathing and emotion is referenced. In addition, some of our published recordings have been reproduced in textbooks.

## DRAMATIC ADIEU TO THE PIGEON WORLD

For another two years, my research on human emotional patterns was carried out parallel to our work on pigeon vision. By that time our laboratory had become part of the Neuroscience Institute and most of our colleagues were concerned with neural processes at the cellular or molecular level. Another group of studies concerned cognitive processes and cerebral modeling, with the use of complex computer programs.

I became increasingly attracted by my research on human emotions. However, it was a difficult theme to be accepted by the CNRS, surrounded as I was by biologists and microchemists on one side and by experts in Artificial Intelligence on the other. What had emotions to do with all this? The time, place and academic atmosphere imperative in the Neurosciences in those days was not yet ready for a more integrative and multidisciplinary approach to the study of emotions.

Although my position as "Directeur de Recherches" (Director of Research) gave me great autonomy, the financial resources of the Institute favored more fashionable subjects, which was definitely not the area of emotions, a subject matter considered to be restricted to clinical psychologists or, as some of my colleagues ironically told me, a subject for poets....

So, rather tired of my scientific double life, I decided to cut it short. In 1991, a German colleague and I organized an International Conference held in Bielefeld, Germany, where distinguished specialists in bird vision around the world would meet and exchange their experiences. The three-day Conference was named "Birds, Vision and Behavior". The 25 selected participants of the "Pigeon Club" (including myself) began enthusiastically to prepare our respective presentations with slides, transparencies, discussions and so on.

> When it was my turn, I presented a synthesis of our research on the frontal and lateral viewing of the Pigeon. At the end of my presentation, carried out according to all the rules of academic/scientific games, I asked the president of the session to allow me a few extra minutes from my discussion period (for those who are not acquainted with these intricacies, it corresponds to a limited period where participants ask, criticize and comment on the presentation), because I wanted to share with my colleagues a matter that was close to my heart. I said that despite my long-time dedication to the pigeon subject matter I had just presented, and that had occupied my scientific activities for so many years, the moment had arrived when I felt the need to respond to a strong urge that had been impelling me for some time towards a different area of knowledge. I expressed it literally as written here.
>
> Among the audience were some young colleagues who knew about my parallel scientific interests. So I invited everyone in the room to watch some video images I had selected to give them a glimpse of what my new interests were. Without further explanation, the image of a lake (Lake Konstanz) in southern Germany, appeared on the screen, with the sound of a voice in the air (my voice) reciting parts of Hamlet's "To be or not to be" monologue. This was immediately followed by a wide shot of the writer (me), sitting on a rock facing the lake, reproducing the Effector Patterns of each basic emotion. The next image showed me again sitting on a rock with open arms, saying with a big smile, "This, my friends, is my goodbye to the pigeon world." Cut. Silence.

The president of the session looked somewhat puzzled and said something about me being an actress and a scientist, after which he opened the discussion period. Immediately a colleague asked a specific question about the pigeon's frontal viewing. Without hesitation I recovered my "scientific persona" and responded with some new data and a few extra slides. After a few other exchanges on the subject my time ended and the next presenter took my place.

During the coffee break, a few colleagues, who made different comments, surrounded me. I asked one of the young German scientists, who was a follower of our work on pigeons, what he thought about the closing of my presentation. He said he had never had a chance to see one of his —so to speak— "scientific mentors" present future research plans so openly and frankly. Another colleague, a professor from New York of my generation, whispered to me discreetly as he passed by my side, saying, "It takes a lot of courage to change at our age!" I was told that later, a group of colleagues stayed at the bar until very late, discussing my daring epilogue to my presentation. Apparently I had defenders and detractors....

I have told this story in detail and exactly as it happened. I recognize that my intervention was provocative and totally unusual, but I do not regret it. On the contrary it helped me to mark a milestone in my life. One is obviously scared, has stomach pangs, vacillations and moments of insecurity. However, to give a step forward in the direction of one's wishes is liberating, although the price is often high. It resulted in my working "counter current" for more than four years on a "high risk" subject, as it was termed by my peers in a written report about my scientific activities at the CNRS. Back in my laboratory in Paris, I consciously and systematically disassembled all the apparatus and paraphernalia, which we had used in our work on pigeons. My pigeon associate, Carlos Martinoya was retiring that year, so I left our young students under other guidance. I felt that my career in animal experimentation had been fulfilled and closed, and that I had finally convinced the CNRS of the validity of my new experimental line of research on human emotions.

*"All's well that ends well!"*

## STRUCTURED REPRESENTATION OF THE BASIC EMOTIONS

One day two students from the Artificial Intelligence Department of the University of Pierre and Marie Curie came to our laboratory to study the Emotional Effector Patterns of the basic emotions as a subject for a special report. They wanted to systematize and identify the prototypical characteristics of each basic emotion, using an "expert system" of analysis. For instance, if the breathing patterns of a certain emotion have a given set of characteristics, the facial muscles another specific functional role, and the postural attitudes could be defined, emotion X would be fully represented. This ensemble of prototypical characteristics, particular for each basic emotion, was represented in the form of a "decision tree."

I was invited to a Symposium in Amsterdam entitled *"Breathing, Voice and Movement"*, organized by the Free University and I decided to present these results that showed the Emotional Effector Patterns in a structured way for the first time. The manuscript was later published in a paper entitled *"Specific respiratory-postural-facial patterns are related to basic emotions."*

> I remember that the day after the symposium, which had been attended by a very heterogeneous audience of physiotherapists, medical doctors, scientists, psychologists and dancers, among others, a journalist who had also assisted, interviewed me for a radio program. We talked freely and at a certain moment she told me of an interesting experience she had had using my method. She said that right after my talk, which had ended with a small demonstration of some of the patterns, she went to telephone her husband. It turned out that they were in a very conflicted relationship and had not been able to communicate for several weeks. Every time that she was determined to approach him in an agreeable way, anger filtered in and she could not control it. Then she remembered the breathing pattern of tenderness that I had demonstrated and before placing the coin in the public telephone, she began to breathe in that way, relaxing her body, smiling slightly and tilting her head a little to one side. Immediately her voice became soft, she said hello to her husband in that mood and was able to establish a quiet and good conversation with him!

I mention this anecdote because it shows in practice what the method can attain. The mere change in breathing and the conscious adoption of a relaxed posture and facial expression modified her emotional state and, as a consequence, her voice changed. The husband-listener on the other end of the phone line received an open communication in a friendly voice, and responded immediately in kind.

One may argue that the journalist had simply decided to be friendly. However, she had tried to do this unsuccessfully many times before. What happens is that if there is anger, the body does not easily obey orders or suggestions coming from the mind. But, direct precise physical respiratory actions, and not a mere mental wish, were capable of immediately producing the physical change that then induces a different emotional state, in this case one of tenderness.

## THE OBSERVER RECOGNIZES WHAT HE SEES: IS SUCH JUDGMENT VALID?

I truly believe, sustained by my friend Humberto Maturana's ideas, that **the observer's judgment should be taken as a scientifically valid element, particularly in the study of emotions**.

I will explain myself. If the emotional respiratory patterns that we found **really** correspond to the studied emotions, a naïve observer should clearly recognize what emotion has been triggered by the correct reproduction of such patterns.

For such judgment to become scientifically valid, it is not sufficient for it to be casually issued. For example, at the beginning of our study, my friend Carlos entered the experimental room and saw a girl crying. Very concerned, he asked the girl what had happened and whether he could be of any help, completely unaware of the fact that she was one of our students who was simply reproducing the Effector Pattern of sadness.

For the observer's judgment to be accepted as scientifically valid, it must be formulated in a structured context, under a rigorous experimental protocol, with a significant number of replications, and with statistically valid results. Such are the rules of the scientific game.

Following these rules the Chilean psychologist, Nancy Aguilera, worked in our laboratory in Paris on a thesis to verify that the correct reproduction of the Effector Patterns of a particular emotion, in fact transmitted the corresponding emotion to the observer.

The formulated hypothesis was the following: if in fact the prototypical Effector Patterns have been correctly defined, independent experts judging their reproduction should be in agreement about the quality of the reproduction. On the other hand, if the Patterns contain all the elements necessary to transmit the corresponding emotional message, even naïve judges should be capable of correctly recognizing the emotions thus generated.

The experience was carried out by showing naïve observers (here called judges) ten-second, silent, video clip sequences, in which subjects are seen reproducing the six emotional patterns. The judges had to identify which emotions were presented and give a degree of certainty for their responses. The accuracy of the rates reached almost 90%, with high levels of certitude when the clips represented patterns that were very well executed. However, correct identification and certitude of judgment dropped to 68 % when the sample of clips had not been selected for high quality in the execution of the patterns.

The results validated the prototypical features of the emotional "Respiratory-Postural-Facial" patterns, showing that they effectively correspond to what people generally recognize in such expressive emotional behaviors.

The experiments and the thesis were later written up in an article which was published, after the usual turmoil, in the *European Bulletin of Cognitive Psychology* (volume 12, n° 2, 1, 1992, pgs. 173-188).

## ANALYSIS OF THE SUBJECTIVE CONTENT OF AN EMOTION

The most difficult aspect of this experimental study is to be able to take the contents of the subjective reports people give after reproducing the patterns, and communicate them scientifically.

One of our French graduate students, Sylvie Paulet, wrote her thesis on the analysis of the degree of subjective activation (feeling) that the experimental subjects had felt when reproducing each of the six emotional patterns.

In order to evaluate the intensity of the induced emotional experience, each subject was asked to evaluate it on a scale of 0-5, ranging from no feeling to most intense feeling. These self-evaluations were then compared to the observers' (judges') judgments, also using the same scale. Once these evaluations had been carried out, the subjects could freely express what they had felt.

These spontaneous reports were classified into three groups:

a) The subject reported having "felt" the emotions corresponding to the pattern, e.g. "I felt very sad" or "I began to get angry."

b) The subject reported mostly physical sensations, such as prickling in the arms and hands, sweating, oppression in the chest, a need to act out physically, but reported no emotional feeling.

c) The subject reported having evoked images or memories connected with the reproduced emotion.

What is interesting in this experimental study, which coincides with multiple reports we have obtained in workshop situations, is that as people practice the patterns, the corresponding feelings become more precise, and what I have called "parasite emotions" start to disappear. This is important for the analysis of mixed emotions, and with practice, helps people to clarify what they are really feeling.

The results of this study were partially reported at the *VIII Conference of the International Society for Research on Emotions* (ISRE), which took place in Cambridge, England, in 1994.

## PUBLISHING IN *THEATRE TOPICS*

In one way or another, the experiences I had accumulated in experimenting and applying this method with actors began to attract the attention of the North American theatre community.

In 1991, I was invited to the Annual Conference of the Association for Theatre in Higher Education (ATHE), which annually assembles faculty members of University Theatre Departments in the United States.

> The talk I gave was entitled, "**New Emotional Freedom for Actors: Discoveries for Helping Actors to Summon and Control Feeling**" a title suggested to me by the organizer of the session, Robert Barton, Director of the Acting Program of the University of Oregon.
>
> The presentation was given in a panel mode. It was received with much interest and was followed by a very vivid and rich discussion with the audience.

As a result an invitation followed to write an article for *Theatre Topics*, a journal edited by the ATHE (Association for Theater in Higher Education). I wrote it and sent it, but stumbled again into the problem of specialization and sacred professional territories.

As it was an atypical contribution the editorial board sent my carefully edited article to several external reviewers. I later received eleven review pages with comments from different consultants (anonymous, of course), full of objections, questions, and requests for clarification on the most varied aspects of the original manuscript. So I rewrote the article and it was finally accepted.

> **As I read and re-read this article, and others read it too, I realize that it expresses far beyond my conscious intentions, the emotional power that develops in the inter-active play between the method and the actor.**

This always brings me back to the scene in Shakespeare's *Hamlet*, where the prince hires a theatre troupe to perform before the court a play representing the murder of his father by his stepfather. In this famous monologue, Hamlet says he is impressed that the emotional expressions of the actors' theatrical representation could be so much stronger and express so much more fiercely the horror of the crime, than what he himself was able to feel.

> *Is it not monstrous that this player here,*
> *But in a fiction, in a dream of passion,*
> *Could force his soul so to his own conceit*
> *That from her working all his visage wann'd,*
> *Tears in his eyes, distraction in's aspect,*
> *A broken voice, and his whole function suiting*
> *With forms to his conceit?*
> *The play's the thing*
> *Wherein I'll catch the conscience of the king!*

(*Hamlet*, Prince of Denmark, Act II, Scene 2)

## THE ARTICLE IN *SCIENCE & VIE*

It is important for experimental findings that have practical applications, to become known to the general public through simple language, thus moving beyond the narrow channels of the scientific community, whose jargon often is unnecessarily complex.

Requested by the French monthly journal *Science et Vie* to contribute to a special thematic edition on emotions, I sent an article called, "*Felt emotions, reproduced emotions*". In this article I used color photographic illustrations and original recordings of the respiratory patterns that could easily be understood by an outsider. They looked —as a young actor-musician once said to me— like musical transcripts!

Whatever, the case may be, I believe I actually succeeded in communicating our findings in colloquial and attractive language for the French speaking reader.

This time there were no editorial difficulties. The article had been requested by the Journal. However, in an attempt to preserve an aesthetic style, my collaborator, filmmaker Pedro Sándor, Sándor, and I intervened in the layout of the article and in the presentation of the original photographs and graphics, besides making suggestions for the final printed format.

> *Ir y quedarse, y con quedar partir,*
> *partir sin alma, y ir con alma ajena,*
> *oír la dulce voz de una sirena*
> *y no poder del árbol desasirse.*
> *To depart and to stay, and by staying, depart,*
> *To depart without soul, and leave with another's,*
> *Hearing the sweet voice of a siren*
> *Unable to detach from the tree.*

(Sonnet LXI, by Lope de Vega)

# PART II
# SCIENCE AND EMOTION

*En dos partes dividida*
*Tengo el alma en confusión*
*Una, esclava a la pasión.*
*Y otra, a la razón medida*
*Guerra civil encendida,*
*Aflige el pecho importuna:*
*Quiere vencer cada una,*
*Y entre fortunas tan varias,*
*Morirán ambas contrarias*
*Pero vencerá ninguna.*

In two parts have I my soul divided in confusion
One part a slave of passion
The other to measured reason-
Bloody civil war afflicts the heart,
Each wanting to conquer,
And among such varied fortunes
Both will die in contradiction,
And none will conquer.

(Sister Juana Inés de la Cruz)

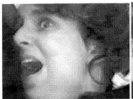

**A**lba Emoting is, as mentioned previously, **a scientific discovery with its derived technique and method, that confirms experimentally the direct and reciprocal physical connection between Breathing and Emotion.**

Therefore, it involves a different way of approaching the relationship between the Psyche (the Mind) and the Body, establishing new ways of handling emotions in any area of human endeavor.

The typical questions that always arise in the mind of people coming into Alba Emoting's fields of action are the following:

- Why is it called *Alba Emoting*?
- Of what does the method consist?
- How does one learn the technical parts?
- Does one need to be an actor to learn it?
- How can a non-robotic use of these patterns be achieved?
- Are basic emotions always brief?

And so on and so forth.

In one way or another, these and many other questions that arise around *Alba Emoting* are answered explicitly or implicitly throughout this book. Another question I am always asked is why I have named this system *Alba Emoting*.

**ALBA** because it is the Dawn, the Aurora. Also in Spanish it means white, and therefore "pure." Alba is not an acronym, as some North Americans initially thought.

**EMOTING** is derived from the seldom used English verb "to emote," that one day unexpectedly occurred to an American colleague with whom I was collaborating, and which means "giving expression to emotion."

I now invite the reader, to learn first about the scientific foundations of this system, and then to see how it can be learned and applied.

# I. SCIENTIFIC FOUNDATIONS: DISCOVERING THE EMOTIONAL EFFECTOR PATTERNS

I shall present here the origin and development of the experiments which led us to demonstrate the existence of certain physiological parameters (such as breathing, heart rate, muscular tone) that are selectively activated during the manifestation of each of the six basic emotions and which contribute to their differentiation.

## FIRST EMPIRICAL OBSERVATIONS

Our initial observations came from clinical work. My Chilean colleague Guy Santibañez had observed in his clinical practice that patients with anxiety syndromes presented clear modifications in their breathing, at the precise instant when they were relating episodes of their lives that were particularly charged with emotional content. If he then asked them to maintain a regular and calm breathing rhythm while they repeated the same painful memories, the patients reported that in doing so, they felt less anxious.

These preliminary observations gave us the first indication of the existence of a particular link between a kind of breathing and a subjective emotional evocation.

Although the relationship between breathing and inner states is at the core of knowledge that comes to us from the Orient –yoga practices to name just one–, to our knowledge no scientific studies had yet been attempted to measure and establish this link systematically.

So, in order to approach the problem scientifically, it was first necessary to find a way to provoke an emotional state under laboratory conditions.

It is not possible to carry around a recording machine in order to find an opportunity to "measure" what happens physiologically in a person that is experiencing an intense emotional moment in real life. At most, it is possible to film it, but then we can only record the external expressive manifestation of the emotion.

Emotions in real life belong to the one who "lives" them, so recording the event in images should only be done with his or her consent. In some cultures the mere act of taking a photograph of a person is to "steal his soul." There are ethical implications when doing research on emotions.

Another problem is trying to record physiological changes present during relatively natural emotional situations, which obviously stop being natural once they are reproduced under arbitrary and artificial laboratory conditions. It is necessary to provoke an emotion experimentally in the laboratory at a precise moment when all the recording paraphernalia is available.

How to proceed? The situation is not what occurs for instance in a psychotherapy session, where the emotion emerges from what the patient is relating. Neither can one provoke the emotion with an external stimulus, like suddenly pushing the person's chair abruptly or saying something violently in order to provoke anger. Not only is this procedure unethical, more so, it is non-specific, as reactions to the same stimulus may be very different with different persons: one may laugh if the chair is pushed away, and another may feel scared or angry.

In order to attempt significant and valid physiological recordings, it was necessary not only to induce an emotion, but it had to be a specific one (sadness, joy, fear, etc.,) with a precise and well-defined beginning and ending.

The first step in the direction of our research was to observe what happened when a person is in a self-induced emotional state. To this purpose, we invited students from the Department of Psychology and from the Theater School, to come to our laboratory at the Physiology Department (Medical School, Universidad de Chile) in Santiago.

We asked the students to lie comfortably on the floor and relax, and to try to remember or relive situations in their lives in which they had experienced a strong emotion. As their evocations developed, some visible external signs began to emerge: one student would slightly open his mouth, another would tense her hands, or give a sigh, while still another would press her eyelids. We took careful notes of the observed physical manifestations, and then asked each subject to roughly describe the evoked emotional memory.

We soon began to realize that there was a good correlation between particular physical manifestations and the kind of emotional experience reported. For example, if someone had evoked a fearful situation, it coincided with an opening and tensing of the eyes and a change in the breathing rhythm. On the other hand, a slight smile and a relaxed body accompanied a pleasant memory.

It became evident that these preliminary observations, carried out during the simple evocation of a personal emotional situation (what is called "emotional memory" in acting techniques based on Stanislavski's Method) were limited to what we could record visually or photographically (video was not yet available). Moreover, the evoked emotional states lasted an indefinite period of time and it was not clear precisely when they started and when they ended.

On the other hand, we realized that the subjects could not always clearly report what they had "felt" during the evocations and that most often emotions were mixed.

## EXPERIENCES AND RECORDINGS UNDER HYPNOSIS

Obviously the reported qualitative observations were insufficient for the rigorous study we had undertaken. We needed to record some of the physiological manifestations that occurred during an authentic emotional state, under controlled conditions.

We therefore decided to use hypnosis which, despite not being a natural state of consciousness, makes it possible to recreate real emotional situations lived by the subject in a controlled temporal course.

The emotional re-creation begins and ends at the precise moment the suggestion is made, and is then suppressed by the hypnotizer. Such a procedure also has the advantage that the same emotional memory can be evoked many times without the interference of the process called "habituation," which consists of the attenuation and eventual disappearance of a reaction by a continuous repetition of the stimulus.

In daily life, someone tells a joke that makes us laugh. If he tells the same joke a second time, we laugh less and if repeated again it is not funny anymore. The same occurs with memories that have a strong emotional charge. A memory may be evoked several times but with repetition, it will little by little eventually lose its emotional power and will slowly fade away.

However, under hypnosis, even the repetition of a strongly charged emotional memory will preserve its intensity and vivacity, as if the person is really living the original situation. In this way it is possible to obtain repeated physiological recordings during a funny situation or a fearful evocation as many times as necessary for reliable measurements.

Taking into account the care that is required when using hypnosis as a technique for emotional induction, and aware of the ethical responsibility inherent in such a procedure, we selected as experimental subjects students who volunteered, that were psychologically well balanced and at the same time good subjects for hypnotic suggestion. We then proceeded to carefully analyze their emotional history, in a similar manner to the way a medical doctor records a clinical history for each patient (anamnesis). We took special care to explore the memory of life situations which had a strong emotional impact and were related to the basic emotions we were exploring.

To carry out these experimental sessions, a standard procedure was developed, as illustrated in the following case:

> The experimental subject (in this case a 22 year-old woman, here named NN) was placed on a couch. External electrodes were attached to record her heart rate, arterial pressure, skin temperature, and muscular tone. A belt, specially adapted with a strain gauge was used to register the movement of the diaphragmatic muscles and/or the thoracic movements, in order to determine her respiratory rate. Once she was lying on the couch with all the recording equipment in place, we proceeded with the hypnotic induction.
> 
> We then said to NN something like "At this moment you are facing your aunt who is scolding you harshly," an episode which we knew from her clinical history was charged with memories of anger. NN immediately accelerated her breathing with ample thoracic movements, her heart rate increased, her eyelids tensed, her jaw contracted and her general muscular tonus increased, especially in the arms and legs, while she lifted her fist as if to strike.
> 
> We let this behavior take its natural course for about 40 seconds and then suggested to her that the situation with her aunt was over and that she was again calm and relaxed. NN instantly relaxed her

tense body, began to breathe evenly again and little by little her heart rate reverted to basal levels.

After a while we suggested a situation from her life which had evoked great anxiety. This time the breathing immediately became very irregular and apneic, with prolonged inspirations. Her mouth and eyes opened tensely and a significant increase in heart rate was recorded. After about 30 seconds, we again instructed a calm state, and the physiological and expressive activation provoked by the reliving of the conflictive situation ceased immediately, with all recordings regaining basal level.

In order to evoke joy we referred to a joke she had told us before. Merely asking her, "Do you remember the joke about the Portuguese?" triggered a loud burst of laughter, with staccato exhalations through her open mouth, teeth fully exposed, eyes partly closed and body relaxed, except for the stomach muscles that were agitated by the violent spasms of the diaphragm. Again, after a few seconds we suggested resuming a calm state. Her breathing immediately recovered a calm rhythm and its basal level.

Short staccato inspirations through the nose, muscle relaxation and tears followed the suggestion of sadness, with return to basal levels as soon as the suggestion ended.

To analyze the physiological and expressive changes that occur during a sexual evocation, we suggested to NN that she was making love with her partner. It is important to mention that we knew from our interview prior to the experience, that she had a normal and satisfactory sexual relationship with him, without fear or inhibitions. She immediately responded to the suggestion with a change in breathing; she threw her head back and started to make sinuous movements with her pelvis. Her face expressed unmistakable pleasure. Once again, after about 30 seconds we suggested the calm state, which she adopted immediately.

Finally, for the emotion of tenderness we suggested that she was holding in her arms her baby niece, whom she loved very much. The suggestion worked immediately. Her breathing became slower, a smile lit up her face, and a glow appeared in her eyes. Her head tilted slightly and her body became totally relaxed. In this condition her heart rate slowed down.

It is interesting to mention here that tenderness is the only basic emotion during which the heart beats slower…

***"Breathe tenderness"*** became the slogan with which scientific and medical participants concluded a Congress on Asthma in France, after my presentation on the "Emotional Effector Patterns." They were quite surprised and very interested to realize that by simply changing one's breathing to a slow rhythm with long exhalations, accompanied by a slight smile and a slight tilt of the head could evoke an emotion of tenderness. I strongly believe that the practice of this simple physical action could be very useful in the treatment of asthmatic patients who have such serious respiratory disorders, often related to emotional problems.

The above-mentioned "Emotional Effector Patterns" were later replicated, recorded, and quantified in a large number of experimental subjects, and the results have been published in international scientific journals, one of which is appended to this book. (See Appendix I)

The ensemble of these observations and measurements confirmed experimentally the existence of a direct link between a special form of breathing, accompanied by particular postural and facial expressions, with the evocation of a corresponding emotional feeling.

A brief explanatory parenthesis: accustomed to so many years of writing scientific articles for the academic world, using a dry and precise language that does not allow poetic flight, I am attempting here to do the opposite, to write with as much expressive freedom as possible, without losing the scientific vigor.

And a poem by Federico García Lorca, comes to my mind,

*Duérmete, clavel*
*que el caballo no quiere beber.*
*Duérmete, rosal,*
*que el caballo se pone a llorar*

Go to sleep, daffodil
the horse does not want to drink.
Go to sleep, rosebud
The horse begins to weep

## WE FEEL WHAT WE BREATHE

The famous French poet, actor and writer, Antonin Artaud, wrote in his essay *Le Theatre et son Double*, published in 1938:

> "*Le souffle accompagne le sentiment et on peut pénétrer dans le sentiment par le souffle, à condition d'avoir su discriminer dans les souffles celui qui convient a ce sentiment.*"

> "Breathing accompanies the feeling and it is possible to enter into the feeling through breathing, **provided one is able to discriminate among the different kinds of breathing, those which correspond to each feeling.**" *(my emphasis and translation)*

I feel in a certain way that our experimental findings with the breathing patterns provide a scientific support to Artaud's poetical assertion, **since we were able to record and discriminate among the different kinds of breathing, those which corresponded to particular feelings.**

### *How do we breathe these basic emotions?*

Of all the physiological changes that occur during an emotional state, breathing seems to be most important as it "draws out," so to speak, other physiological changes.

For instance, breathing through the open mouth at a rapid frequency of about 1-2 cycles per second is quite different from breathing through the nose with a rhythm of 3-5 cycles per minute. Different physiological, biochemical, hormonal and many other reactions occur in the organism. The entire cardiovascular system is in close connection with the respiratory system, so it is evident that if I intentionally change my breathing, many other reactions in my body over which I have no control, will also change.

Breathing is a vital function that has two precise characteristics, one that is mechanical and essential for life —we breathe without being aware, without thinking about it— and another which we can handle consciously. It is only humans who have this special capacity of being able to actively and intentionally change our breathing modifying at will the size and frequency of our diaphragmatic movements, regulating the tension of the intercostal muscles and modifying the duration of the respiratory "pause."

We have the possibility and capacity to decide in an instant to breathe more slowly, to hold our breath like when we swim underwater, or to accelerate our breathing rhythm to prepare for exerting a strong physical effort.

We can also train ourselves to handle our breathing habits better.

> If we wish we can breathe softly,
> Rhythmically,
> Slowly,
> In peace.
> We can also sigh at will…

We may thus conclude that since our experimental results show that **a particular form of breathing corresponds with and distinguishes between each of the six basic emotions,** our Emotional Effector Patterns provide a scientific support to Artaud's genial poetical assertion.

The following chart represents the description of each respiratory pattern in the form of a "decision tree."

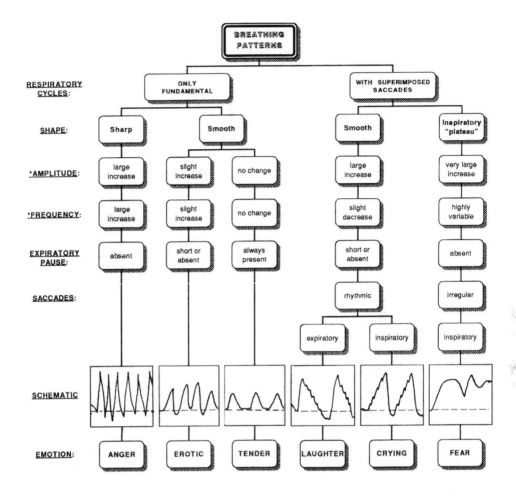

## BODY POSTURE AND FACIAL EXPRESSION

In the same way that we can regulate our breathing at will if we train ourselves, we can also modify our gestures, body positions, the degree of muscle tension, the position of our extremities, our walking speed, how we sit or stand. We can similarly change the expression of our faces, erase our frown, relax our jaw, and smile. Any healthy person, with no training, is capable of saying, "I will now contract my right foot" or "I will make a grimace" or "I shall hold my breath."

There are very few studies that have analyzed in detail the characteristic body attitudes that correspond to different emotional states. Our observations of breathing patterns gave us the first clues of the corporeal elements that characterize the different emotions we studied.

We began to analyze specifically the body actions that a person could modify at will, since our interest was to develop a physical tool that would allow people to get in contact with their own emotions at will, in a simple and direct way. This meant to learn to consciously coordinate all three levels of an emotional state: organic, expressive and subjective.

The research also aimed at allowing me to fulfill my passion for the theatre, since I was seeking a formula that would help actors to create emotions onstage without becoming trapped in or overwhelmed by them.

## *How does the body move in different emotional states?*

> *The soul yearns to live in the body because*
> *without the body it can neither act nor feel.*
> (Leonardo da Vinci)

From our initial experiences, we developed observation protocols for the expressive roles of postural and facial expressions. Two parameters were essential for the analysis of the expressive role of posture: the muscular tension/relaxation and the forward/backward body balance.

In order to systematize the elements we found in our study, I am presenting here the six basic emotions in a graphic form: a vertical axis that represents the degree of tension/relaxation, expressing maximal to minimal muscular tone, and a horizontal axis for the degree of approach/retreat, which illustrates the basic tendency to lean forward or backwards.

# POSTURAL AXES

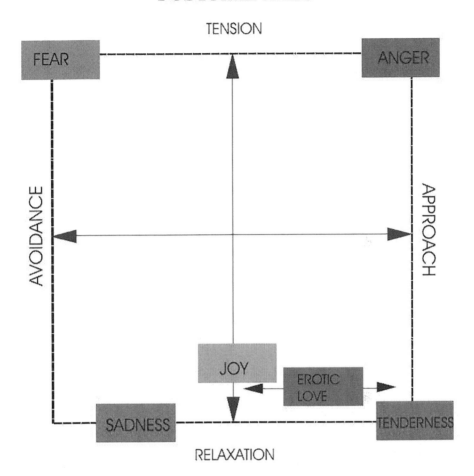

As shown in the figure, anger and fear are the emotions in the position of maximal muscular tension, but with opposite directional attitudes: approach, for anger (the person is prepared to attack) and retreat/avoidance for fear, (the person prepares to run away or remains tensely immobile, depending on whether his behavior involves active or passive fear).

With differing degrees of relaxation, are placed sadness, tenderness, (parental love, friendship) erotic love (initial stage of sexual arousal), and joy. These four emotions however, are expressed with different directional attitudes: slight downward recoil for sadness (the person closes-up); a somewhat vertical posture (open, head slightly backwards) for joy: an attitude of more or less accentuated approach in the case of sexual attraction, depending on whether the expression is of a more active or more receptive nature; and finally, an attitude of full approach in the case of tenderness (the person prepares to touch, caress, protect).

The prototypical postural features – degree of muscular tension, quality and type of movement, directional body posture and head orientation are summarized on the following "decision tree."

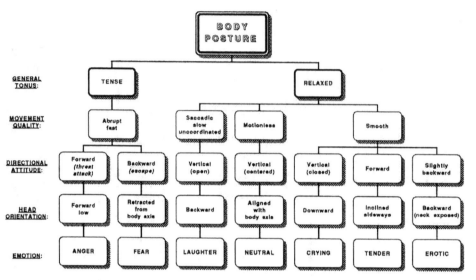

*Figure 2: Prototypical features of body posture for each emotion: general tonus, movement quality, directional attitude and head orientation.*

## What happens with our faces when we emote-

Like breathing and posture, the face is also a dual system. On the one hand it shows expressions that may be adopted deliberately. On the other, it presents infinite and continuous changes of which the person has no awareness, but which are visible and can be recognized by the external observer.

The face as a means of communication is even more important than the body because, in our culture, when we talk to someone, we usually look at his or her face. Moreover, the gaze is very important, especially the expression of the eyes which have been described as being "Windows of the Soul."

There are in fact over 300 very flexible facial muscles, including those that regulate eye movements, which are the fastest movements of the human body. The main function of most facial muscles is to provide mobility and expression to the face.

The next figure presents, once again in the form of a decision tree, the main facial features which characterize each basic emotion: to what degree the eyes open, the degree of tension of the eyelids and the brow, the position of the eyebrows, where the gaze is directed, and the mouth-lips configuration. Photos of the typical facial expressions have been added.

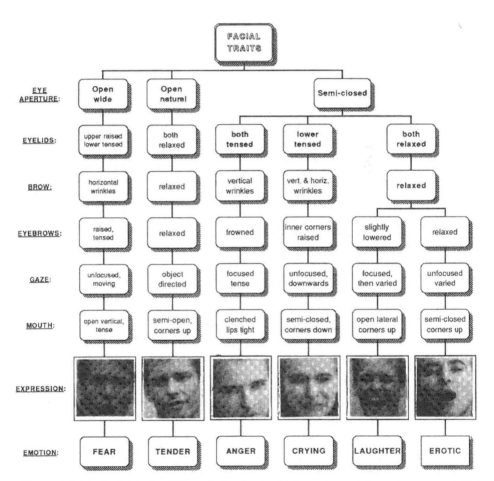

*Figure 3: Main facial traits differentiating each emotion: degree of eye aperture, position and/or degree of tension/relaxation of eyelids, muscular tension of the brow, direction of gaze, mouth/lips configuration and examples of typical facial expressions.*

# II. THE EMOTIONAL EFFECTOR PATTERNS

## RESPIRATORY-POSTURAL-FACIAL PATTERNS

From the complex ensemble of physiological reactions that occur during an emotional state, we extracted from our observations and experimental measurements those elements that can be controlled at will, regulated by the striate muscles (so-called voluntary muscles) the breathing rhythms, the facial expressions, the body attitudes (gestures and posture).

We gave these respiratory-postural-facial combinations, prototypical for each basic emotion, the name of *"Emotional Effector Patterns."*

I shall now present the specific characteristics of these patterns for each emotion[1], illuminated by some literary quotes.

The graphs are examples of recordings of respiratory movements for each basic emotion, and were recorded from experimental subjects. The vertical axis ("abscissa"), calibrated in millimeters represents the extent of thorax expansion, and the horizontal axis (the ordinate), represents the breathing rhythm (the frequency of respiratory cycles). The upward arrows indicate inhalation.

---

1 There are readers who can interpret these descriptions of the Effector Patterns adequately —especially those who have experience with motor-kinesthetic or vocal disciplines— and who can therefore "enter" into the corresponding emotion by following the procedures described. However I do not recommend doing these exercises without an expert to teach them at the beginning. It is a simple but powerful technique and it requires certain knowledge to be able to handle it.

## Joy-Laughter

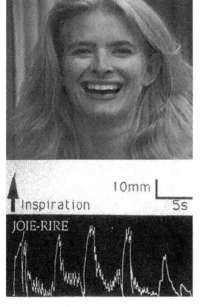

*Hay muchas maneras de dividir los seres humanos—le dijo- . Yo los divido entre los que se arrugan para arriba y los que se arrugan para abajo, y quiero pertenecer a los primeros. Quiero que mi cara de vieja no sea triste, quiero tener las arrugas de la risa y llevármelas conmigo al otro mundo. Quién sabe lo que habrá que enfrentar allá.*

There are many ways to divide human beings. I divide them into those who get wrinkled upwards belong to the former. As an old woman, I don't want my face to be sad. I want to have the lines of joy and laughter and take them with me to the other world. Who knows what I will have to face there.

*(Mujeres de Ojos Grandes, "Women with Big Eyes" by Angeles Mastretta)*

Laughter is the extreme expression of joy, and it is this we have recorded. The main respiratory characteristics are a brief and abrupt intake of breath through the nose, followed by exhalation through the open mouth, the air being expelled in small explosive exhalations that may even invade the respiratory pause. The outer sides of the lips are pulled naturally to the sides as if emitting the "ee" sound in English, (like in "cheese"), thereby exposing the teeth. At the same time, the eyes get smaller, because when the lips are stretched sideways, the orbital muscles contract. In fact, in spontaneous laughter, this last characteristic is essential for recognizing joy in a face because if it doesn't occur, even if the mouth appears to be smiling, the observer will immediately realize that something does not quite fit and will perceive a mixed emotion. This is the example of the famous "false smile" that has been very well described by Paul Ekman.

In the case of extreme joy, when expressed by authentic natural laughter, the person is more centered in herself, momentarily somewhat disconnected from her surroundings. This is the reason why the body posture is neither forward, towards the stimulus, nor backwards as if avoiding something. If a postural direction can be characterized for a big laugh, I would say that people typically oscillate around the vertical axis, slightly pulling back, with eyes partly closed and unfocused. At an extreme intensity one may drop to the floor as muscles relax.

## Sadness-crying (Weeping)

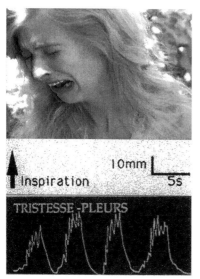

*Camposanto no, camposanto no, lecho de tierra, cama que los cobija y que los mece por el cielo. Quítate las manos de la cara. Hemos de pasar días terribles. No quiero ver a nadie. La tierra y yo. Mi llanto y yo. Y estas cuatro parede!*

Cemetery no, cemetery no, bed of earth, bed that protects them and rocks them through the sky. Take your hands off your face. We have to spend terrible days. I want to see no one. The earth and me, my weeping and I, and these four walls!

(From *Bodas de Sangre, Blood Wedding* by Federico Garcia Lorca:)

Weeping is the expression of extreme sadness and the respiratory pattern that characterizes it is opposite to that of laughter. The saccadic respiratory movements in weeping interrupt the inhalation phase of breathing. The air enters in short saccades, also through the nose, followed by a long exhalation through the open mouth (as in a sigh). When weeping increases, these saccadic outbursts may also invade the expiratory phase of breathing.

In sadness the body is relaxed and yields to the pull of gravity. A kind of bodily lassitude accompanies these convulsive and spasmodic movements of the diaphragm during the entire breathing cycle. The body is felt as heavy, it curves, the head hangs down and the eyesight is directed downwards; the eyes are semi-closed and unfocused. There's a frown on the brow and the eyebrows are slightly elevated at their inner extremes. Movements are slow and heavy; one walks with difficulty. There is a tendency to lie down, to cover one's face and do nothing.

## Fear-Anxiety

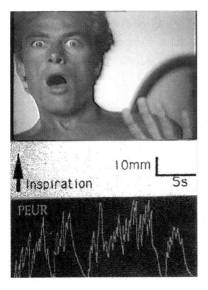

*All those lost fears are here again. The fear that a strand of wool that hangs from the edge of the bedcover is as hard and as sharp as a steel needle; the fear that a certain number will begin to grow in my head until it no longer has a place in me; the fear that I may betray myself and tell of everything that I fear, and the fear that I may not be able to say anything, because everything is unstable, and those other fears... The fears.*

(From Rainer Maria Rilke, a German-speaking Czech poet who lived from 1875 to 1926. This is an excerpt from his terrifying *Malte Laurids Brigge* notebooks.)

Fear is essentially a reaction to a dangerous situation. There are two possible visible manifestations of fear: the active fear that prepares the organism for flight and the passive fear that is characterized by a reaction of total immobility of the body, which freezes as if paralyzed. Basically a person with fear tries to avoid a dangerous situation, be it real or imagined. In both types of fear there is great generalized physiological activity. The heart rate increases noticeably and the postural aspect of the effector pattern is characterized by a massive increase in muscular tension. The breathing pattern shows periods of very brief inhalations, —an apnea-like breathing— (which is almost as if breathing has stopped), followed by passive incomplete exhalations and sometimes by an expiratory phase like a sigh. This respiratory characteristic can appear during a normal respiratory cycle, or can be maintained during several breathing cycles, and as a result develops into the irregular breathing which characterizes a person who is anxious or chronically afraid.

Facial expressions are characterized by a large increase in tension of most of the facial muscles; the eyes are wide open, exorbitantly open and the pupils become dilated. This typical characteristic is adaptive because it makes it possible to enlarge the visual field and therefore creates a more panoramic view of what is happening, allowing the person to see better where the danger is and where to escape.

In the Effector Pattern which corresponds to passive fear (a kind of freezing reaction), the body remains immobile in a position where the shoulders are very tense, the neck is brought in as if avoiding something, and the arms and hands are lifted in a kind of self-protective gesture. This passive response has a very ancestral origin.

There are animals in the jungle that remain totally immobile, as if dead, when a very powerful predator is approaching. Stage fright is a typical example of passive fear. Actors or speakers or simply employees who are terrified in the face of authority may suddenly remain totally immobile, tense, hardly breathing, with the saliva drying, forgetting what they had to say or unable to articulate the words. To this is added, of course, the physiological reactions of the total Effector Pattern, which, in the case of fear, is especially characterized by strong tachycardia (increase of heart rate) even when the fear is passive and is immobilizing. The child who hides under the sheets for fear of a monster coming is another example of this tensely passive fear reaction, in this case, triggered by an imaginary situation.

In active fear the body posture is modified by a compulsive reaction to run away and therefore it is another set of muscles that contract, as the organism is mobilized for flight. Panic attacks (which occur so frequently nowadays, with people living in large cities) typically present with some of these expressive signs that I have just mentioned, among others.

When fear has no clear real cause and is sustained in time, we call it "anxiety." If we observe a person who is anxious, we will see that she/he presents the same effector patterns that have just been described, although maybe in a more subtle form. Even if the somatic manifestations of body posture and expression are the same, what changes in the case of anxiety is the situation that provokes the reaction: it is generally purely mental, (psychological) and therefore learned during the course of life. In fact, most people who say they are anxious frequently don't know why. The fears described by the poet Rilke belong to this kind of fear that has no apparent real cause.

## Anger-Aggression

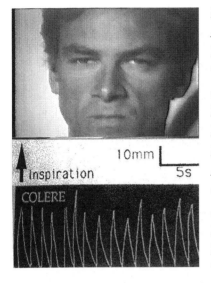

*In peace there's nothing so becomes a man*
*As modest stillness and humility:*
*But when the blast of war blows in our ears,*
*Then imitate the action of a tiger;*
*Stiffen the sinews, summon up the blood,*
*Disguise fair nature with hard-favour' rage;*
*Let it pry through the portage of the head*
*Like the brass cannon; let the brow o'erwhelm it*
*As fearfully as doth a galled rock*
*O'erhang and jutty his confounded base,*
*Swill'd with the wild and wasteful ocean,*
*Now set the teeth and stretch the nostril wide,*
*Hold hard the breath, and bend up every spirit*
*To his full height!*

(William Shakespeare, Henry the Fifth, Act III, Scene 1)

The breathing pattern that we recorded for anger is characterized by cycles of high frequency and great amplitude. (In workshops I always describe this breathing as being ragged, as the "teeth of a saw.") Inhalation and exhalation take place through the nose (nostrils dilating and contracting abruptly). Facial muscles are in tension. The jaw is contracted, the lips and teeth are clenched, and the eyes are tense, because the upper and lower eyelid muscles contract. The gaze is totally focused on the point of attack ("if looks could kill"). This aspect is very important in the expression of anger because when we focus our gaze, we use the part of our retina which is richest in receptors (the fovea) and allows us to have the best visual clarity of the object of our rage.

Muscular tone increases in all muscles of the body, particularly in those used in the posture of attack. Fists are contracted as if ready to hit. The entire body, especially the head, goes forward, the neck is contracted and the veins bulge visibly (like a bull ready to attack).

# Erotic love – Sexuality

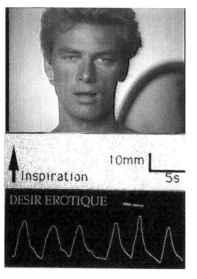

*Cuando enmudece tu lengua,*
*y se apresura tu aliento.*
*y tus mejillas se encienden,*
*y, entornas tus ojos negros.*
*por ver entre tus pestañas*
*brillar con húmedo fuego*
*la ardiente chispa que brota*
*del volcán de los deseos,*
*diera alma mia*
*por cuanto espero:*
*¡la fe, el espiritu, la tierra, el cielo.*

When your tongue gets mute
And your breath accelerates
And your cheeks flush
And your black eyes turn,
to see between your lashes
as they shine in humid fire
the ardent sparkle that erupts
from the volcano of desires.
I would give, my beloved,
for what I expect,
the faith, the soul,
the earth, the heaven!

(Gustavo Adolfo Bécquer)

The principal respiratory trait of sexual activation consists of a relatively regular rhythm that increases in intensity and frequency depending on the degree of intensity of the sexual impulse and subjective involvement. Breath comes through the open and relaxed mouth, with a slight smile on the face. Facial muscles are relaxed, eyes are partly closed. In the receptive version of the Erotic Pattern, the head is slightly tilted back and the neck exposed.

The general distribution of muscular tone corresponds to a posture of approach in a relaxed attitude. Nevertheless, the abdominal muscles will augment their tonic activity, depending on the intensity of the sexual arousal and will present phasic, synchronized discharges.

During lovemaking, the Effector Pattern is executed in dynamic postures with rhythmic movements of the pelvis, which increase in frequency as the climax is approached.

The pattern that has been described corresponds to the active sexual behavior in lovemaking which goes *in crescendo*. Nevertheless, the respiratory effector and expressive patterns are also present, although much more subtly, during flirting, at the moment when two people look at each other and are sexually attracted.

### Tenderness-Parental love-Friendship

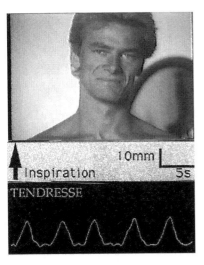

*Tu pupila es azul, y cuando ries,*
*su claridad suave me recuerda*
*el trémulo fulgor de la mañana*
*que en el mar se refleja.*

Your pupil is blue and when you smile,
its soft clarity evokes in me
the trembling glitter of the dawn
reflected in the sea.

(G.A. Bécquer)

The respiratory pattern is characterized by a very calm rhythm of inhaling and exhaling through the nose, very regularly and with low frequency of breaths. The mouth is closed; the lips are relaxed forming a soft smile. The muscles of the face are all very relaxed and the head is slightly tilted to the side. The whole behavioral attitude is one of approach. Part of the active emotional pattern of tenderness is softly touching, caressing, and feeling with the hands. Vocalizations that are emitted are like lullabies or soft sounds or murmurs.

Tenderness is the only basic emotion of the six that we have measured, during which there is a decrease in heart rate. The heart beats slowly and rhythmically, accompanying the slow and regular exhalation of the breath.

Tenderness is a state of peace, of internal and external relaxation. The gesture in the expression of tenderness is toward the other. It is a behavior that is expressed towards someone else– towards a child, a friend, a comrade. It is the emotion of friendship, parental and fraternal love. I mention here a childhood memory as an example:

> *"When my father every morning took me to school in Santiago, –I must have been about 10 years old– I wore a very short skirt that didn't cover my knees. This was a German tradition. I very clearly remember that the bus was very, very cold and that my father, in a protective gesture, covered my legs with half of his coat. The trip lasted about an hour and during that trip he was teaching me geography, like in a game. He used to say, 'Imagine you are traveling from Madrid to Berlin.' And I had to tell him the rivers, mountains, valleys, cities through which I would travel on this voyage...."*

While I remember this now, many, many years later, I lift my head, I slightly incline it to the side, a soft smile appears on my face; I feel that my eyes get slightly moist, my body relaxes and my breathing becomes soft and calm.

I don't know if this feeling corresponds to what I felt then, but even today that memory evokes in me a deep tender feeling.

If somebody of any nationality or race entered my room at the moment I was experiencing this emotion, they would perceive this expression of tenderness in me. It is clear that we are talking here about expressive codes of communication that are universal and atavistic.

# NEUTRAL (NON—EMOTIONAL BREATHING)

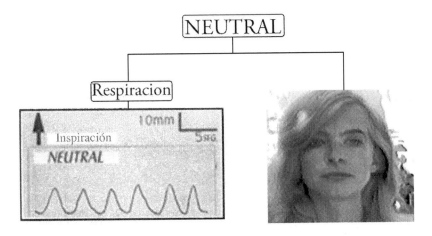

Neutral breathing is characterized by a calm and regular rhythm: the air enters through the nose and is slowly exhaled through relaxed lips, with a tiny opening that will allow the air to come out as if the person were inperceptively blowing out an imaginary candle. Inhalation and exhalation are approximately of the same duration, so that the recording of the respiratory movements looks very much like a sinusoidal wave.

The facial expression should be as neutral as possible with eyesight focused on a point in the distant horizon. Facial muscles are very relaxed. The body is erect and the feet are solidly planted on the floor, with their external borders parallel and separated by about a foot's width, so that the external lines of the feet are parallel to the external parts of the shoulders.

This pattern which I have called "Neutral" provides a starting point for any emotional pattern and which should be returned to after finishing an emotion, as we will see later when describing the "Step-Out Technique."

Another interesting observation made during this work with emotions, is the difficulty that people have in reaching a truly neutral emotional state. In fact, most of the time when people try to be neutral, expressive characteristics of the most frequent emotion of that person filter through. It is as if the traits of the personality begin to take possession, especially on the face. Such traits —all the expressive traits of the emotions that are most important in the life of that person— leave strong traces over the years. This is why older people who are, for example, easily angered or people who have a rather depressed nature, present in their expressions as they try to be neutral, the prototypical features of those emotions which have dominated their character all their lives.

**In summary, through the results of our research and experience in training people with the Alba Emoting system, we were able to confirm the particular respiratory configuration and the typical expressive somatic patterns that are characteristic for each basic emotion.**

# III. ALBA EMOTING: A NEW METHOD FOR EMOTIONAL INDUCTION

We can now ask ourselves what is the practical utility of the discovery of these prototypical Emotional Effector Patterns, aside from their purely scientific interest. Our findings undoubtedly contribute to the understanding of the complex world of emotions.

But more so, as frequently occurs in scientific research, something unprecedented happened. As the study progressed, the discovery of the Effector Patterns led unexpectedly to the creation of a new and original method for Emotional Induction.

## EMOTIONAL INDUCTION: PROCEDURE TO "ENTER" INTO AN EMOTION

Once the typical respiratory-postural-facial patterns for each basic emotion were clearly identified, we decided to see what happened if we taught a person –uninformed as to the intention of the exercise– (a person who in scientific jargon is called a "naïve subject"), to reproduce these same patterns intentionally under precise instructions.

Right from the start, we observed that if the person followed the instructions to reproduce, let's say first the breathing pattern of fear and then add a certain tension of the face muscles, regulating the degree to which the eyes are open and adopting a body stance of withdrawal, in a few minutes the person would begin to feel close to a state of anxiety.

If, on the other hand, we would instruct the same person to breathe with the anger pattern –obviously without mentioning the name of the emotion–, asking him to contract muscles that would induce a posture of attack, his facial expression would unmistakably start to show signs of anger. If we questioned him at the end of the exercise, he would say that he had begun to get quite irritated and had evoked a personal situation in which he had experienced anger.

Repeated experiences with the reproduction of different Emotional Effector Patterns showed us that the corresponding emotions were induced in total absence of any external stimulus or situation, which could have provoked such an emotional reaction.

**This means that the mere execution of the specific Effector Pattern of an Emotion could produce a subjective response in the person and the emotional "color" would correspond to the effector configuration that had been reproduced.**

The concrete procedure for inducing emotions in this way was the following:

We asked the subject to breathe very calmly, with a regular rhythm, relaxing all facial muscles, with the eyes open looking straight to a point on the horizon and to adopt a centered posture. This baseline condition corresponds to a neutral non-emotional state, which I call "zero level" or baseline. Then we gave instructions for a particular breathing pattern in very precise but colloquial terms. For instance in the case of anger, the instructions were as follows:

> *"Breathe through the nose with fast abrupt intakes of breath and exhalations. Keep your lips tight and clench your teeth. Continue this breathing and start to contract your shoulders, arm muscles and neck. Bend your body and head slightly forwards,"* and if necessary, because these actions often develop naturally, we added: *"Contract your jaws, frown, tense your eyes and focus them on a nearby point."*

These instructions were very precise and were repeated and/or elaborated slightly according to the efficiency with which the subjects followed them. Often, just a few well-reproduced breathing patterns were sufficient for the other aspects of the Effector Patterns to appear. After about 1 or 2 minutes, the person presented all the expressive signs of the induced emotion. In the above case it was anger or at least irritation. After giving instructions to end the exercise and a normal breathing rhythm and relaxed posture were re-established (i.e. returning to a base level or what I have called Neutral), we asked the person to report what he/she felt. The great majority of subjects said that they had started to get angry. The intensity of the reaction depended on the duration of the exercise.

We repeated the same experimental protocol with the Effector Patterns of each of the six basic emotions: joy-laughter; sadness-weeping; fear-anxiety; anger-aggression; sexuality, and tenderness.

In short, our study systematically confirmed that the accurate reproduction of the respiratory-postural-facial pattern of a particular basic emotion triggers in the person images, sensations, feelings and/or memories related to that emotion. **Therefore, it is possible to induce a genuine emotional state by reproducing the corresponding precise and specific physical actions, in the absence of any real or imagined external situation.**

**This is *Alba Emoting*.**

I will now relate the experience I had with Julian, an actor from Spain who came to visit his friends one summer during which we were holding a workshop in the south of France. He knew nothing about the method and arrived in a very happy, relaxed mood. We asked him if he would participate in an experience and allow my associate Pedro Sándor to film it.

Once Julian was comfortably settled in a quiet room, I asked him to be as relaxed as possible and to breathe calmly, keeping a neutral attitude. Then I gave him the following instructions:

> *"Please start to breathe through your nose, with short saccadic intakes of breath followed by a long exhalation through your open relaxed mouth. Relax your body, feeling a certain heaviness; drop your head and direct your gaze downwards; keep your eyes partly closed and try to lift the inside ends of your eyebrows. Let the breathing guide you."*

Little by little, while carrying out the described actions, his face and his body posture started to display an expression of deep sadness and tears began to well up in his eyes. After a while, I decided to interrupt the exercise by asking him to return to his initial calm breathing; to touch his face gently and to change the position of his body. He needed at least a full minute to recover and return to his initial relaxed mood. When I asked him what had happened to him, he said he had relived a very painful moment in his life.

Later on he confessed that if I had not stopped the exercise, he would have "wept all the tears of the world!"

122　THE ALBA OF EMOTIONS

I report this experience in detail because, since it was filmed in real time and never edited, it has allowed me to illustrate the induction procedure step by step. In fact, I have shown the unedited sequence –which by now is over 15 years old– to several different people, both privately and in conferences, to academic as well as to general audiences. It always provokes a profound sympathetic response. People are "moved" by witnessing the entering into sorrow of an adult man who simply follows the instructions to reproduce an Emotional Effector Pattern.

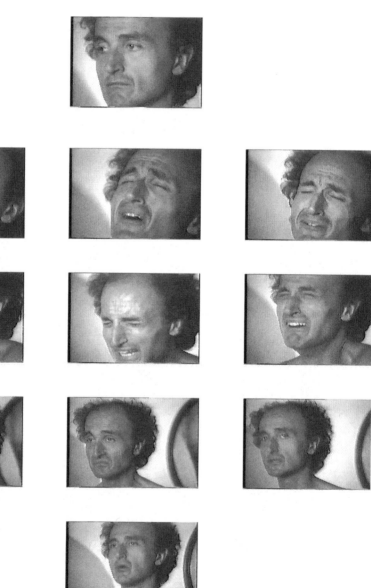

In fact, as I have already mentioned, the intentionally reproduced actions, which at the beginning seem very technical, very soon start to integrate organically with the subject's own emotionality.

So, even if at the beginning the instructed patterns look as if they were carried out very mechanically, (in fact, I have called this first phase of the induction process, the "robotic phase"), as the person continues to breathe in the indicated pattern, little by little it becomes more natural, as if the person's own respiratory system had entered into a "resonance" with the imposed rhythm.

The same thing occurs with the facial and postural expressions. In fact, it is at the precise moment that the entire emotional pattern is organically integrated, that the person connects with his/her own emotion.

Something quite special occurs here: at the moment the person is doing the exercise, there is no situation –real or imagined– to justify the reaction of fear, sadness, anger or joy that was induced. The person (experimental subject) has simply reproduced following precise instructions, a particular respiratory-postural-facial pattern. There is no external situation or stimulus that could have provoked the emotion.

**It bears repeating, the elicited emotion is triggered by the execution of precise physical actions and not by a real or imagined "emotion-generating" situation.**

We are dealing here with a process of inducing an emotion by an organic activation that starts in the "periphery" or lower part of the organism, and then travels towards the higher brain centers. This process has a feedback connotation and could technically be called a "bottom-up procedure."

Over the years, I have repeated the same procedure, which I described with Julian, the Spanish actor, with many people of different nationalities, ages, and professional backgrounds, basically obtaining the same results.

I am still surprised today by the power and effectiveness of this procedure. The strength and veracity of the evoked emotion always impresses both those who witness and those who experience the induction procedure, whether in workshop or in private session.

Therefore, experiences of this kind also convinced me that the observer's judgment must be considered as a scientifically valid criterion, especially in the study of emotions.

## THE "STEP-OUT" PROCEDURE

One of the things we very often observed at the beginning, when using the described Emotional Induction Procedure, was that the "induced" subjects tended to stay "trapped," as it were, in the induced emotion, as frequently happens in daily life. Therefore, for example, after carrying out the pattern for sadness, the person would leave the laboratory with a feeling of sorrow or had sad dreams that night. Since we followed up closely on the actors and students that were our first experimental subjects, we were fortunate in being able to make this very important observation right at the beginning of our studies.

In order to avoid this effect, which I have called "Emotional Hangover," it became necessary to deactivate the induced emotion by carrying out a reverse procedure. We needed to develop a kind of "step out of the emotion," a technique that would enable the subject to return to a neutral emotional state, attentive to the exterior world but fundamentally centered and maintaining a very regular and calm breathing pattern.

But how could one learn to handle and control such a useful and powerful tool?

From my own experience in working with different body techniques and meditation, I developed a specific technique for "stepping out." This roughly consists of ending each pattern reproduction with at least three complete slow, deep and regular breathing cycles, followed by complete relaxation of the facial muscles and a change in postural attitude.

### "Recipe" for the Step-Out

**Stand in an upright position with feet parallel, aligned with the hip bones, facial muscles relaxed and eyes open looking straight ahead at the level of the horizon. In this posture, you breathe in through the nose and out through the mouth with a quiet, easy and relaxed rhythm, without forcing the breath, trying to keep inhalations and exhalations equal in time. The respiratory rhythm is then synchronized with a continuous movement of the arms: while inhaling, the extended arms are lifted in front of the body, with hands interlocked loosely, tracing a sort of "generous arc" over the head, bending the elbows as the hands reach behind the neck. During this action, inhalation is synchronized with the speed of the lifting arms.**

Then, after a brief pause, the air is gently expelled through slightly open lips (as if blowing out an imaginary candle), while the arms descend in synchrony with the exhalation, until they return to the initial position. At this moment all the air must have been expelled. This cycle is repeated at least three times, very consciously. Then the face is gently touched, both hands giving small massage-like movements, from the center of the face outwards. Finally, the exercise is concluded by shaking the whole body and then changing posture.

This "Step-Out" exercise acts as a kind of "reset" or back to "base level" of the emotional excitement, and allows the person to return to a neutral state. It takes a longer or shorter time, depending upon the degree of intensity reached by the emotional induction. For example, if a critical level of emotional activation has been reached, especially the first time one does these exercises, it is best for the induced emotion to follows its normal course and manifest in its total, often dramatic, reality. However, it must necessarily be followed by the step-out exercise, which must be repeated until all traces of emotion have disappeared.

Mastering this simple technique is essential for those who work with **Alba Emoting**. It provides the user with a tool that makes it possible to return to a neutral, non-emotional state at any moment, attaining what I call "emotional silence."

Such a technique can also be used in daily life after any strong emotional reaction. Personally, I recommend practicing "Step-Out" as much as possible, especially in life situations where a disturbing and unwanted emotion creeps in when we need to be calm.

Sometime ago I received a message from my friend, sociologist Elena Moreno, after she had read a first draft of a chapter for this book:

*"I can tell you, Susana, that for me the Step-Out, while learning **Alba Emoting**, was as powerful as what I discovered with meditation in my spiritual world. How can I express it? To find that little key which is capable of stopping the emotional flow, has been in my existence as important as discovering that I can vacate my mind of thoughts, judgments, and vagaries and simply be alive. I have the feeling that the "Step-Out" is the base on which all six basic emotions can be constructed. Without going through the "Step-Out," it would be impossible, (I think, maybe I am wrong) to experience the emotions in their most pure state.*

*I have lately had the opportunity to observe my grandchildren who, as you know, are babies. The youngest is only 7 months and is very expressive. He cries when he is sad, shrieks with anger and laughs openly. Between one emotion and another, he breathes in a quiet and regular way, stares at a certain point in space, and looks as if he were absent. I tell my daughter that he is in "step-out"... My granddaughter who is two years old has already learned to talk and spends less time in Step-Out, although it is still an important part of her existence. To recover the Step-Out is to recover part of our innocence and I hope that in your book you stress this point because it was you who taught me this possibility. The six emotions are the chromatic tones and the seventh is* the light and like in a painting, it is white. Valdivia, the city in southern Chile where I now live, is a city of painters and the artists say that they draw colors from darkness because here, this is seen in the landscape. One day it is dark and there are no colors; then suddenly a ray of light filters through the overcast sky and the river that looked black becomes green, blue, violet ... Personally, when I am upset and my emotions are mixed and confused, I feel muddy, obscure. The step-out exercise is like introducing a ray of light that emerges from that paused breathing. The body in a harmonious, balanced posture, the gaze calmly focused on a spot straight ahead, makes it possible for emotions to clear and the rainbow to appear after the storm, when it is still raining and the sun gives us a wink. If you make the analogy between emotions and colors, think of this, all colors mixed on the palette result in black and the experts define black as the absence of light. An excess of stimulation confuses us emotionally and we feel stressed. Too many mixed emotions produce stress and we end up acting like robots, with our feelings frozen. In the midst of turmoil, a simple exercise with Alba Emoting enables us to catch our breath and to contact the present moment, where there is a time and place for everything. Dedicate a space in your book to the "Step-Out," so that humanity can recover a bit of its innocence, and we shall all be grateful.

With love and respect,
Elena

***Alba Emoting* induces an emotion from physical actions and steps out of an emotion, through physical actions.**

**This is *Alba Emoting*.**

# FROM THE TECHNIQUE TO THE METHOD: RECOMMENDATIONS TO LEARN ALBA EMOTING

It is very important to realize that the technical part of this method could be learned by any person, simply by imitating the patterns that show the respiratory recordings, published in scientific articles, or through the experience of someone having taught them to you.

However, and **I insist, it is essential that this learning be done under the guidance of an expert**. In spite of the fact that the method deals with a technique that is apparently very simple, it requires precise adjustments of the facial muscles, the body posture, and especially of the breathing. This cannot be learned by simply reading an article about the procedure, or vicariously from the experience of another person who learned it during a workshop.

Since the reproduction of the patterns triggers genuine emotions, an inexperienced person doing the exercises, without expert guidance could enter into an uncontrolled state of anxiety or of depression, especially when using the patterns of fear or of sadness. This is why I insist on the need to first learn the step-out technique so as to avoid possible uncontrolled emotional reactions. With practice, *Alba Emoting* makes it possible to learn to induce controlled emotional states and to be able to leave them consciously at any moment.

The entire procedure for learning the method is described in Part III: Training Actors.

On the other hand, in order to avoid robotic use of the emotional patterns, the expert teacher must not only have experience with the method, but must also teach it with a strong ethical conscience. This is equally true for the learner.

With these principles in mind, let me respond to the question of how to avoid a robotic use of the technique.

The process of learning *Alba Emoting* does not resort to psychological evocations, emotionally stimulating situations, or external elements such as music or pictures. First and foremost, it is basically using the particular breathing pattern followed by the corresponding posture and facial expression that induces the emotion and makes it possible to step out of it. It is important to remember that all exercises are carried out with eyes open, so that the person always remains lucidly in the present and aware of the surroundings.

During workshops, the participants start by learning the neutral state already described, which corresponds to the step-out. Once it has been learned, each emotional effector pattern is taught and practiced. This is done with the help of texts, everyday actions, and situations from personal or professional life, and all kinds of interactions with other participants, always within an ethical and esthetic framework. **There is no cathartic process involved.**

In short, the method allows any person to generate, control, modulate, alternate, and mix different basic emotions, thus helping people to handle better the ever present universe of mixed emotions in which we usually live.

# SCIENCE AND EMOTION 129

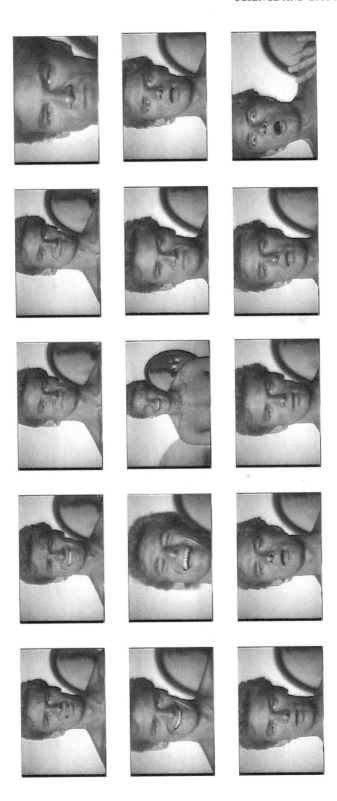

# PART III
# ADVENTURES OF THE AUTHOR
# WITH HER METHOD

# I. IN THE THEATRE WORLD

The work with actors, the development of exercises and the general procedure to teach the method have been an essential part of my scientific-artistic venture.

With this method I have been able to re-live my interest in the theatre intensely and passionately. It has proved to be particularly useful for acting, directing, as well as for establishing the "emotional melodies" of theatrical texts.

It somehow connected me with my youthful ambition to study acting, a goal that was cut short by the anxiety I developed after seeing how often actors became possessed by their roles in a way that seemed to me rather unhealthy.

However the method that I developed, aside from providing a systematic way of working professionally with emotions, **also protects actors psychologically, helping them to avoid what I have called "emotional hangovers."**

## STORIES LIVED WITH THEATRE PEOPLE

**Etelvino Vásquez**, director of the Teatro del Norte, Asturias, Spain wrote the following letter to me in April, 1992. I have translated it and include it here:

> "In the summer of 1989, I went to Saintes (France) to participate in a Seminar entitled, "Theatre and Life Sciences," organized by Jean Marie Pradier. There, I met Susana Bloch and joined her workshop on emotions. I was surprised to see that Susana could teach me some cues, some models that allowed me to access emotions without the need to visualize events from my

life by using my guts as my sole inspiration. This was something I had been seeking for a long time. Until then the only resource I had at hand was emotional memory, which I often realized just ran out of the power to inspire me.

What were for me until that moment only simple "babblings," intuitions and perhaps a little more, began to take shape in me in a triple sense, as an actor, as a director, and as a teacher, from that encounter with Susana. (Since 1986, I have been the teacher of Interpretation at the Theatre Institute, in Asturias, Spain.)

As an actor, I tried to be as rigorous as possible with myself in learning and applying the different emotional patterns. It was required to control the face, the mouth, and mainly the breathing, and not only for acting during performance but also during rehearsals. I found that the body was nothing without the emotions and the voice, even in the pre-expressive situation of training. This is what I tried to communicate to my companions. Susana Bloch's method turned out to be for me as a director not only a great tool for analyzing texts (also a fundamental part of the work of an actor), but also a means to work with the actor-character's emotions without the need to enter too deeply into complex, unmanageable emotional memories.

From the director's chair I could see if the Emotional Pattern was done well or not, since so very often actors tell me that they feel the emotion, but are not capable of embodying it using the right physical gestures, expressions and breathing.

The success of my production of [Perfume de Mimosas] by Miguel Murillo with the [Compañía Extrema Suripanta], was undoubtedly a result of the knowledge I got from Susana. This show was very successful in this country, traveled twice to America, and won a prize in Venezuela. As it was a play strongly based on emotions, I cannot separate its success from the great help Susana's method gave me for directing it.

As a pedagogue, I try to explain in my classes —as clearly as my experience with this method permits— what happens with the six basic emotions based on their prototypical respiratory-bodily patterns, insisting all the time on the close relation between body, voice, movement and text. I notice that students tend to offer a certain resistance, probably because they consider emotions to be something very private and subjective, and think that they only appear by magic — how far away they are from the reality of acting!— but I am certain that with time and practice, they will understand perfectly well what seemed so far away from their inner world during their student years.

When Eugenio Barba speaks about the Biological Principles that govern the "life" of all actors: balance, opposition and simplification, he obviously forgets a fundamental principle, at least for western theatre, and that is the alteration of breathing. Without this alteration there can be no emotion. Physiological emotional changes are also present in the actor's body as it goes from an everyday life condition to a state of representation on the stage.

I believe that with Susana Bloch's **Alba Emoting** method, the actor using the patterns can attain a much more technical mastery of a particular emotional expressivity which will then give him more liberty to "act" freely. It will allow him to access the emotional world more rapidly and with greater security, without the need to constantly resort to emotional memory and introspection.

It is undoubtedly a first-rate tool for stage directing as it provides perfect knowledge of human emotional behavior, and I dare say that without such knowledge, it is not possible to direct.

At this point, my knowledge of the **Alba Emoting** method is still very limited and I find it difficult to develop it by myself. It is essential to have a good teacher and individual training. Since Susana Bloch's application of her method is just beginning, it is urgent for her to train experts in this method rapidly, so that it can become incorporated in theatre schools' curricula, and in a few years become a necessary daily tool for actors."

**Felix Rellstab**, Director of *the Schauspiel Akademie Zurich, Switzerland:*
By the end of the eighties, I met Felix Rellstab, actor, dramaturge, teacher, creator and director of the prestigious German-speaking Theatre Academy, *Schauspiel Akademie, Zurich*. Talking about theatre over a cup of coffee, I mentioned my experiences with actors and emotions, and gave him my article, *"Emotional Effector Patterns: a Psychophysiological Method for Training Actors"* that we had just published in the *Journal of Social and Biological Structures*, and that summed up our first experiences with the method in Chile.

A year after this encounter I received a letter in Paris from Rellstab in which he told me that while he was clearing up his desk, he found my article that had been mislaid among other papers, and read it, finding it very interesting. He proposed that he come to Paris and meet me there, to find a way to start collaborating.

From that moment on, for many years, I went regularly to Zurich to work with the Emotional Effector Patterns with the students and also the teachers at *the Schauspiel Akademie*. Felix Rellstab attended some of my workshops as a "regular student." He later organized workshops for me with professional actors, and began to introduce the **Alba Emoting** method in his own rehearsals and classes.

Some years later Rellstab published an article in German entitled: *"Konstantin Stanislavski: Neue Aspekte und Perspektiven"* (*Konstantin Stanislavski, New Aspects and Perspectives*). In this article he refers to our work as a new approach to the actor's process of emotional recreation. Since he, himself, had experienced **Alba Emoting**, he wrote:

> *"The person reproducing the Effector Patterns not only evokes the corresponding emotion, but also sees images popping out; one begins to evoke emotion-related situations, pictures emerge, yes, they actually emerge!"*

In the last years of his life —when I met him he was over 70— he continued to include **Alba Emoting** in his classes and in his writings. He devotes an entire chapter in the first volume, *Grundlagen*, of his *Handbuch Theaterspielen*.

**Joan Polvsen,** Danish actress, an expert practitioner and collaborator at the very early stage of this method:

Joan told me that she had been invited by a well-known Danish film director to participate as an extra in a film. The scene included a large group of people laughing. Since the weather was very bad and rainy the day of the shooting, it took over eight hours, and the extras had to maintain, somehow, the required emotional state throughout, while waiting for the rain to stop. When the session finally ended, the cameraman came running directly towards Joan and told her that she and her companion were the only ones among the 100 extras who could sustain the mood of laughter for such a long time. He could clearly see this through his camera and wanted to know how she did it. Joan answered, "It is **Alba Emoting!**"

She told me later that what she had done, in fact, was to instruct the person next to her to do the laughing pattern, and then the two women alternated doing the effector pattern and telling each other funny things, and that every time they lost the mood, they would redo the respiratory pattern and off they went giggling again.

This example is particularly interesting, because it seems that for actors, joy is one of the most difficult emotions to sustain convincingly when performing.

**Horacio Muñoz,** Chilean theatre director, founder of the Teaterklanen, in Denmark:

Much of the theatre work we have done with the method has been filmed by Pedro Sándor. I remember in particular and vividly his filming when Horacio was directing a scene from Chekhov's *Uncle Vanya*, with two young Danish actors trained in **Alba Emoting**.

The scene was rehearsed several times while Pedro filmed the entire process with camera in hand, freely circling around the actors:

The process started with Horacio calmly asking the actress, "*Hanne, what is the basic emotion of your character?*" To which she answered, "*It is a mixture of sadness and tenderness.*" "*Fine,*" answered Horacio, "*Do it.*" Then he asked the same question of Soren, who played the doctor, and he said it was a mixture of anger and fear. Horacio then just told both of them to start with the corresponding Emotional Effector Patterns, and to begin the scene using the respiratory pattern of the dominant emotion. He then told the actors to execute the patterns for a couple of minutes (as if they were "tuning" their emotional instruments) and then after the word, "Action," the rehearsal began. It was just as simple as that, with no confusion, discussions, or complicated psychological explanations.

**Richard Geer,** North American theatre director and theatre anthropologist:

A few years later, when Richard Geer was working on his doctoral thesis in the Department of The Performing Arts, at Northwestern University in Chicago, he became interested in my research on emotions. He came to Paris and spent a month in my laboratory. In the midst of multiple experiences, discussions and materials we were working on, he saw the video of the filmed rehearsal described above, and after seeing it, he wrote the following:

> "*The Teaterklanen was founded in Denmark as a theatre company essentially devoted to putting in practice the* **Alba Emoting** *method. I have seen the results. The actors are not that different from good actors anywhere. The difference is that although the members of the company are very young and inexperienced, they are capable of giving beautifully subtle and complex performances in which the emotions appear subtly or intensely, as the case may be, over a large range of colors and with the ability to make quick changes in the type of emotion or in the intensity of the emotion.*

A filmed sequence of actors rehearsing a scene from Checkov's *Uncle Vania*.

*I remember seeing two second-year actors rehearsing a scene from Chekhov's Uncle Vanya, in which Vanya is drinking alcohol and Sonia joins him in reminiscences. The video flows unedited through several repeated rehearsals of the same scene. After each rehearsal, the director of the Teaterklanen, Horacio Muñoz, makes a few comments. The scene is interpreted with oscillations between laughter and tears; it seems to contain an entire life of hope, anger, and grief, interspersed with short bursts of laughter. The emotions overflowed, and dripped as transparent crystals, like the liquor in Tanya's glass. I was fascinated (captivated), even though they spoke a language I did not understand. It reminded me of myself when I am in a morose and pathetic mood. I am forty-three years old, and they are less than twenty. Amazing."*

## TRAINING ACTORS

Let me briefly describe the procedure with which actors are trained in the method within the context of a theatre school or in workshops. This section deals mainly with the teaching process we developed in Chile with Santibañez and Orthous between 1970 and 1973, with young actors of the Theatre School of the Universidad de Chile. We further developed the teaching process in Denmark with theatre director, Horacio Muñoz, between 1975 and 1985, with his two consecutive theatre companies, the *Rimfaxe Teater* and the *Teaterklanen*.[2]

## *The basic emotional patterns*

Actors were first instructed to adopt a particular breathing pattern without being told the name of the corresponding emotion; then the postural component was added and finally, the facial expression.

The complete configuration was always worked out for each emotion in the same order: breathing–posture–facial expression. The pattern was sustained until a signal was given to stop.

In the beginning each subject would do the exercise individually, sustaining it for about 15 to 80 seconds depending on the instructor's directions. In the early stages of training, it is convenient to prolong the exercise so that the actor may enter fully into the particular emotion; in

---

2 The basic procedure for training the Emotional Effector Patterns I am presenting here is essentially the same to be used with any person in any domain. In the particular case of actors, however the exercises are more oriented to the creation of characters so their training takes longer and is structured more systematically.

other words to experience the subjective activation (feeling) and thus become aware of the effect produced by the exercise.

The procedure is repeated 2 or 3 times, especially with those actors who have difficulties expressing and feeling a particular emotion. An actor may, for instance, have special problems expressing anger or sadness. Then the step-out procedure is taught at the beginning and the actor is instructed to do this exercise immediately after ending the pattern.

He is then asked to describe what he had felt while doing the exercise, whether the actor had "entered" into the emotion, whether particular images had appeared, and, as a whole, what were his impressions.

In the succeeding stages of training, the patterns were initiated, stopped and reinitiated in such rapid succession that subjective involvement was reduced. The entire procedure was therefore very technical and methodical: first the required respiratory pattern was taught, followed by precise instructions to contract and relax specific parts of the body and finally to add the corresponding facial expression.

Interestingly, however we observed in most of the subjects that the facial and bodily expressions appeared by themselves as soon as the prototypical emotional breathing pattern started.

It is recommended not to work with the patterns for more than 2 to 3 minutes, alternating them with other general body work such as stretching, postural changes, a quick game, reciting a brief text, and then coming back for some more work with the patterns. It is very important to work with care and individual attention since controlled respiration and voluntary muscular movements are very tiring and at the beginning very emotionally demanding exercises.

Once each Effector Pattern was mastered, different modulations in intensity, different successions of patterns, and different mixtures were worked out in order to gradually develop the technique into a structured method. Actors could later choose to use this technique for characterizations and for building roles.

If in the process of learning, a particular pattern is not correctly reproduced, the emotional message that is communicated becomes ambiguous, and an observer will immediately detect that something is wrong. For instance, if during the execution of the laughing pattern the person tenses the body, the perceived emotion is not one of joy. Merely changing the amount of muscular tension is enough to correct the pattern, which may then transmit joy.

It is quite probable that spectators of a theatre performance will often detect something wrong or unconvincing in the acting because they somehow perceive, even unconsciously, the lack of organic coherence between the breathing and the expressive components of the emotion.

## *Modulation of intensity*

The patterns were first learned with maximal intensity (i.e. with the maximal muscular activation or relaxation) and with the particular breathing pattern in its most intensive, almost exaggerated mode. Once the pattern was well-practiced at such a level, the intensity was reduced. This was done by giving precise instructions for modulating (decreasing the intensity of the breathing pattern) and for diminishing the amount of muscular tension and/or the number of body and facial muscle groups involved, in a very controlled manner. At least three levels of intensity were practiced, (1) minimal (2) moderate and (3) maximal, until the actors were able to reproduce each at will.

Once the emotional patterns with their basic effector components and different degrees of intensity were well mastered, exercises were developed in which an action or text was modulated with different emotional patterns. Some of the preparatory exercises, such as symmetric and asymmetric contraction-relaxation exercises, and exploratory-cognitive exercises, were practiced with the different learned Effector Patterns.

This was done by modifying the patterns with different parts of the body, for instance doing the "anger" pattern with the corresponding breathing, but tensing only the left arm. Simple actions were practiced with different patterns, for instance carrying a chair with the sadness pattern. In other exercises the actor had to recite a simple poem or speak the lines of a text or sing a song, first in a neutral emotional tone and then while executing each of the learned Effector Patterns.

These exercises prepare the actor for working with mixed emotions.

## *Succession of emotional patterns and theatre games*

The next step was to learn to switch from one pattern to another in quick succession. This was done in the following way: while a pattern was being performed, a signal was given for a quick switch to a different pattern or to a change of one of the components of the same pattern.

This kind of procedure was repeated until the subjects could go easily from one emotional pattern to another. Once this was mastered, the actors, working in couples or in groups, were each assigned a given pattern to start the game with. At the same time, they were instructed to perform an action and to be ready to switch to another pattern at a given signal. At least one normal breathing cycle had to be inserted between each change of pattern.

When the Effector Patterns are mastered, actors can use them at will or under instruction in particular spatio-temporal configurations and under controlled intensities. They can alternate between one emotional pattern and another, perform different stage actions with different patterns, for instance taking a glass with a tense hand and then only relaxing the hand without changing the breathing pattern, or sing a song with the facial expression of joy and then switch only the breathing pattern to sadness.

The resulting changes produced by such actions are immediately and clearly perceived by the observer, and constitute preparatory exercises for working with mixed emotions.

As actors improve in mastering the patterns, they can obtain finer and subtler modulations of expressive intensities. In order to achieve this, as has already been said, it is important to learn the emotional patterns in their maximal intensities at the beginning, so that the actor can enter into the emotional feelings with varying intensities later on.

Let me give an example. The breathing pattern of anger, which is very rapid and intense, may cause hyperventilation and the actor may feel dizzy. In that case the pattern should only be practiced in its most intense form for short periods, not longer than 15 seconds, alternating with other exercises, and always ending the pattern with the described Step-Out technique.

In this intense modality the reproduced patterns may often appear to be "over acted." However, with training, it is possible to obtain more subtle changes in breathing, and more localized muscular tensing, so that actors can learn to reproduce the patterns with less intensity, without losing their particular structure. In this way, with practice, the actor progressively will use the method within a more sophisticated artistic framework, as needed for the creation of a role or a character.

The practice with the patterns also develops a certain sensitization, so that later on a subtle change in the pattern will produce a change in the emotional modality, which is clear to the subject as well as to the observer. This is an important issue since long, sustained emotional output may be required on the stage, in which case the extreme intense version of the pattern should not be maintained.

Any person watching the correct execution of an Emotional Effector Pattern perceives the represented emotion as a real and spontaneous emotion. This is particularly amazing when one observes a sequence of "theatre games" in which trained actors alternate different patterns in rapid successions and combinations.

Isabel Santelices, one of the young actresses trained in the method with Horacio Muñoz and me at the Theatre School of the Universidad de Chile, describes this type of exercise as follows:

> *"The empty stage and four acting students. No situation, no text, no characters. The actors choose an emotion and interact with each other only using the Emotional Patterns. They can change the emotion as wanted, provided the patterns are clearly performed. Little by little a coherent story begins to develop, more or less clear, depending on the actors' sensitivity to playing the game and the clarity in the reproduction of the patterns."*

She then added, referring to her own learning process with the method:

> *"In the four years following my initial learning of **Alba Emoting** I had no direct contact with the technique, however I continue to use it. Often one does not grasp its value at the moment: it needs time to mature. And then, even without realizing it, one begins to "read" life, theatre, photography, etc. differently; one is always observing and comparing everything under the influence of this new knowledge."*

This report followed an entirely arbitrary exercise in the sense that there was neither plot nor text. Nevertheless the pure expressive patterns executed in an unplanned sequence communicated meanings to the observer. If the performers were asked if they had felt the particular emotions represented, i.e. whether they had been subjectively involved, the most frequent answer was that they were only concentrating on executing the instructed patterns as precisely as possible.

This is good evidence that in order to be "natural" or "authentic" on the stage, it is not a "sine qua non" (obligatory) condition that the actor must "feel" the emotion interpreted, but that what is essential is to produce the correct expressive "output" of the emotion.

In my opinion, subjective involvement and emotional identification, if anything, diminishes the theatrical performance, rather than enhancing it.

In this respect I concur with what Denis Diderot, French writer and philosopher, who states in his famous *The Actor's Paradox*:

> "*Tout son talent consiste non pas à sentir comme vous le suposez, mais à rendre si scrupuleusement les signes extérieurs du sentiment, que vous vous y trompe.*"

> "All the actor's talent consists not in feeling, as you suppose, but in rendering as clearly as possible all the external signs of the feeling so that you are deceived."

It is, in fact, possible that actors tend to confuse that general excitement they feel when they are performing with the belief that they are actually **feeling** the emotion they are representing.

## *The "Step-Out" technique*

As I have already mentioned, we observed right from the beginning of our research that the actors, after reproducing the emotional patterns, had a tendency to experience what I have called "emotional hangovers," that is to say, they remained, as it were, "caught up" in the emotion.

This could be particularly disturbing when the induced emotion is sadness, fear, or anger. But we soon found out that by repeating the initiation and ending of the emotional patterns, using a precise "stepping-out" technique, such after-effects were largely eliminated.

A return to breathing in a rhythmic normal state and a change in posture (Step-Out) will immediately modify an internal state. Therefore, the induced emotional condition will return to one that is "neutral."

*One must always finish any exercise with an Emotional Effector Pattern with at least three complete normal breathing cycles and a complete change in posture.* **So, it is essential to use the Step-Out technique almost as a ritual.**

Such a procedure, described in detail in Part II, prevents the actors from remaining in the induced emotion beyond the exercise.

## *Mixed Emotions*

We human beings live most of our daily lives in a state of mixed emotions. This means that pure emotions are rarely present. In fact they are also rare in theatre plays, film or television (possibly with the exception of the Greek tragedies) because pure emotions do not reflect our human reality. In our Western societies sex, for instance, is very often contaminated with anger and/or fear, and anger is frequently accompanied by sadness or is transformed into sarcasm or verbal abuse.

The *Alba Emoting* method allows actors to work professionally with complex mixed emotions. This can be done by combining parts of one effector pattern with parts of another pattern, or by learning to alternate very rapidly between the basic patterns of the mixture.

Let us look at a few examples:

> **Pride** can be described as a particular blend of joy and anger. In order to perform it, the actor can put a certain degree of tension in the body, (anger/intensity degree 1, for example), especially in the neck and back muscles, tilting the head slightly back, while adding a low intensity breathing pattern of laughter/joy.

> **Irony (sarcasm).** Here again the blend suggested is also a mixture of joy and anger, but the proportions in these patterns are different. The instruction to the actor this time is to put some tension in the legs and arms, accompanied by a more intense laughter pattern than in the previous case.

> **Jealousy** is a mixture of anger and fear with a dose of sexuality. To perform this blend actors can slightly tense their bodies while breathing with the anger pattern and at the same time opening their eyes wide, as part of the facial fear pattern. If appropriate to the situation, low intensity sexual breathing can be alternated with anger breathing.

Once this basic "recipe" is understood, each mixed emotion can be worked out, by exploring and finding the optimal proportions of the "basic" ingredients. If an actor, for example, wants to portray despair or powerlessness, which consists of a mixture of sadness, anger and fear, he or she can combine the breathing of sadness, anger and fear in different degrees of intensities, with partial body tension and a degree of the facial expression of fear.

The training with such mixed or alternated patterns leads directly into the preparation of a role. The construction of the Troll scene in Ibsen's *Peer Gynt* (Act 2, Scene 6), –a production directed by Horacio Muñoz in Denmark– was done entirely with mixtures of this kind which created the grotesqueness needed.

The first group of actors who started to use the Emotional Effector Patterns experimentally in theatre performance was those we worked with quite at the beginning of our research, back in Chile. At the end of their training, the actors used the technique in Sophocles' *Antigone*, under the theatrical direction of the great Chilean theatre director, Pedro Orthous.

The text was analyzed in terms of the basic and mixed emotions involved, and the roles were built by putting the method into action. For instance in Antigone's monologue to the citizens of Thebes, the mixed emotion of anger and sadness of her speech was performed by saying the words within the breathing pattern of sadness and adding tension in the neck and leg muscles. The effect was striking, as judged by the audience's rapt attention and reaction.

## *Analysis and notation of the "emotional melodies" of dramatic texts.*

***Alba Emoting*** allows a kind of analysis of dramatic texts in terms of what I have called ***"the emotional melody"***. Such a melody may be established for the entire play, for each character or for any particular scene.

In a theatrical text there is always –as in fact there is in any human behavior– some kind of emotional tone that needs to be analyzed in order to be correctly interpreted, and upon which the emotional melody will flow. This melody corresponds to the particular emotional reactions the character has to develop all through the play.

For this purpose the ***Alba Emoting*** method proposes a rigorous dissection of the text in terms of the required Emotional Patterns needed at each moment of the play. A kind of emotional "score" may thus be established and notated in a clear and reproducible way. I believe such a procedure helps actors and directors to have an objective map of the emotional behaviors present at each moment of the play.

Since quite often the psychological language used in the theatre to depict emotions is imprecise, it seems to me that it would be useful to develop appropriate terminology that would facilitate communication between actors and directors. A kind of semantic reference system could thus be developed that would unify emotional terminology for theatrical purposes, in a sense comparable to the Laban System for movement notation.

## *Collateral Psychotherapeutic Effects*

Just as an actor can use the Emotional Effector Patterns without having to "feel" or relive the emotion represented on the stage, the use of the Effector Patterns can also work well in relation to psychological problems people may have in their personal lives.

One of the actresses we worked with had serious sexual problems in her private life. As she usually mixed feelings of sexual love with those of fear, consequently, she showed great rigidity and body tension when performing love scenes. We worked with her with the sexual Effector Pattern until she could master it. When she learned to use the pattern during rehearsals, she could enact the same love scenes in a much more convincing way.

In this example, if the director would have asked the actress to perform the love scene while thinking about her own sexual life with her husband (emotional memory) the scene would have completely failed to transmit any convincing sensuality.

By using the correct emotional Effector Pattern -in this case the sexual pattern- which organically integrates directly with her own physical sexuality the scene could become much more convincing and real as it will not be tainted by an unwanted personal mixed emotion.

It was very interesting to find in that particular case that learning to use the sexual (Erotic) pattern also helped this actress in her personal sexual life, which as she later reported, improved greatly.

This method, therefore, helps actors to better recognize their own emotions, and face some of their personal conflicts and inhibitions which may become serious professional handicaps. In other words this method increases an actor's skill, by freeing him from the exclusive dependency on his own personal experiences as the source for evoking emotions.

If an actor, when interpreting Hamlet for instance, bases his characterization solely on his own emotional experience (which of course is personal and therefore limited by definition), he will most likely limit the character, who is supposed to be much more universal. If the actor has the opportunity to use a method that allows him to enter into the more universal dimension of an emotion, he may enlarge his perception and the scope of his acting by enriching his emotional mastery. In this way his own self, John or Jim, will be transcended, and the character will really become Hamlet.

I have always believed that if people are not able to express their emotions in daily life, they may be more or less neurotic, but an actor who is not capable of clearly identifying and correctly expressing all emotions, will be professionally limited.

An actor must be capable of expressing and communicating from the stage or on screen any of the vast emotional nuances of the human condition.

**The actor must in fact be, as stated by Antonin Artaud, a true "athlete of emotions."**

## *Resistance to the use of the method: defenders and detractors*

Unfortunately in spite of the interest that ***Alba Emoting*** evokes, it does at the same time generate a certain resistance in the theatre world. In general, actors base their work with emotions on the Stanislavski method, later developed by the Actors Studio, a system essentially centered in living, re-living or remembering the actors own emotions ("emotional memory").

Konstantin Stanislavski, the brilliant Russian theatre director and theoretician, had revolutionized theatrical representation by encouraging actors to completely identify with their characters. It is however interesting to note that at the end of his life, Stanislavski himself recognized that the exclusive use of such emotional memories ultimately produced neurotic actors.

> I remember that during our initial sessions in applying our experiences with actors I got frequent comments such as "I am an artist, and not a guinea pig," or, "I give myself intuitively to the emotion, and science has nothing to do with this."

I do not discuss the validity of such objections, but I have seen in practice that as actors accept the exercises, they begin to realize their utility.

It is only through direct experience with the method that its use and veracity can be grasped. Reading about it in articles or attending conferences is insufficient, especially so for actors, who are basically pragmatic and experiential.

This is what Nancy Loitz, a North American theatre professor, refers to when speaking about my method after she came to work with me during her sabbatical year in 1993 when she participated in the International Seminar on **Alba Emoting**, which I led in Cachagua, Chile. After returning to her university she wrote the following in her report to the Dean of Illinois Wesleyan in Bloomington, Illinois. Here, I include an extract of that report:

> *"The work of Susana Bloch has been criticized by some theatre artists in the United States who have read about her work but have not had direct experience with her method. Those who criticize her work pretend that it is "external" and "superficial." But those of us who have directly experienced the emotional induction and have been able to recreate at will any of the six basic emotions, can testify that* ***Alba Emoting*** *is anything but external and superficial.*
>
> *Besides, as* ***Alba Emoting*** *is not based on the re-creation of emotional moments from the actor's personal lives, it constitutes a psychologically healthier technique for creating intense emotions on the stage. Also a very crucial aspect of the technique is the "Step-Out" procedure, which allows actors to free themselves immediately from the emotion performed and to come back to a neutral emotional state right away. This frees the actors from what Susana Bloch calls "emotional hangover" which is so common with many other methods actors use when dealing with strong emotions."*

I have verified with actors of different nationalities and different degrees of professional experience that the utilization of our method not only provides them with physical technical support for expressing and representing emotions, but also protects them from psychological risks inherent in their profession. Let us remember that a great number of actors enter into roles representing very intense emotional states which they often cannot abandon once their performance is finished.

A North American actress wrote a letter to Richard Geer, a theatre director who was interested in what he called "cooling down" (similar to what I call "Step-Out"), a letter I here transcribe:

> "*Without doubt, the art of acting can be risky for mental health, but until very recently, actors were not aware of such risk or felt unable to face it. With the exception of my late teacher Eric Morris, psychological self-defense was never a topic in our training as actors in any of theatre classes that I have had.*"

Referring to a play in which she interpreted with great success, the role of a bourgeois lady, she said that the character was in her own words: "*so committed to social roles that she goes baloney, throwing out a long racist speech, and ending on the floor babbling over the old, spoiled veil of her wedding dress.*" In spite of the fact that many of the spectators found this ending of the play very real and sincere, she said, "*During the two years acting in the play I was very depressed. Even though I have had long periods of depression since childhood, I had never reached the point of trying to commit suicide. Now, having interpreted this character for so long, I think of dying every day.*"

This report illustrates, as others, the aura of emotional imbalance that frequently surrounds the actor's universe.

I repeat again that the proposed method has the advantage of being based on concrete physical actions that prevent dangerously deep immersion into the actors' own emotions. It provides at the same time a systematic physical way for entering and for leaving an emotional state at will.

Danish actress, Anne Lise Gabold says, "**Alba Emoting allows descent into the depths of an emotional well, knowing that one always has at hand, at any moment, the rope (Step-Out) that can immediately pull you back to the surface.**"

Let us reiterate that **Alba Emoting** allows one to enter into an emotional state by the correct execution of the corresponding Emotional Effector Pattern. It is not triggered through a thought, an image, or a memory. It is therefore a "Bottom-Up" (physically induced) procedure of emotional induction. An intentional change in breath is undoubtedly more precise compared to a rather vague, cloudy memory.

Obviously, to rely solely on the emotions is not sufficient for preparing a role. Actors need to enter into so many other aspects, cultural, historical, linguistic. I am referring here exclusively to what concerns the recreation of emotional states and the protection of the actor's psychological balance (health). In no way will the method replace or diminish intuition, imagination and creativity which are essential to become a fine actor.

## CONCLUSIONS FOR TRAINING ACTORS

The experience that we have so far collected with this method training actors, analyzing dramatic texts and consulting with directors, allows me to formulate the following advantages of **Alba Emoting**:

- a) It evokes emotional expression in a concrete and precise way.
- b) It standardizes emotional terminology, thus facilitating communication between actors and directors.
- c) It helps actors to regulate precisely the different degrees of intensity needed for expressing/accessing the required emotion.
- d) It provides a method for working with "mixed emotions."
- e) It contributes to the protection of the actor's mental health.
- f) It provides actors with a rapid and efficient technique to "Step-Out" of an emotion, thus giving even more protection to their psychological balance, allowing them, at the same time, to master a controlled flow of emotions during a performance.
- g) It helps to eliminate undesired "clichés," allowing the actor to present the physiological parameters that accompany a genuine emotion.
- h) It becomes very useful for text analysis and reduces rehearsal time compared with the classic method of evoking "emotional memories."
- i) It proposes a notation system for the "emotional script" of a dramatic text.

My experience working with actors from different countries in the Americas and Europe confirms that by working with this method a good actor can be even better, and an actor with fewer personal resources will definitely gain in emotional "mastery."

Again it must be stressed here that we are dealing with a technical support for the actor's mastery, which in no way will affect his creativity and imagination. For instance it can only be of help for an actor to know that the degree of eye opening substantially modifies the entire expression of the face, or that in a state of anger the body posture is always leaning forward, as in attack, with tension in the muscles. And that it is impossible to portray joy or tenderness without being relaxed and breathing with long exhalations.

Although breathing is harder to perceive visually than facial expression or body posture, we must not forget that it is the basis of it all: the appropriate gesture without the corresponding breath does not transmit emotion. Adding the respiratory element immediately brings the emotion alive.

**In short, the application of the method in training actors shows that the correct execution of the Emotional Effector Patterns is sufficient to evoke the corresponding emotion in the audience. At the same time actors report that the correct execution of the patterns also may trigger the corresponding subjective feeling in them.**

The results of the training also confirm that with the precise "Step-In" and "Step-Out" of the Effector Patterns, the actor can enter or leave an emotion at will. With this, he attains the ability to perform the expressive components of an emotion that will evoke the corresponding emotion in the audience without necessarily identifying or becoming "possessed" by the character portrayed. And finally, as an additional benefit, the method not only allows actors to control the stresses generated before, during, and after a performance, but may have a psychotherapeutic effect on their lives as well.

## II. IN THE FILM WORLD WITH PEDRO SÁNDOR

*Alba Emoting* can be a great support for filming and the visual arts in general, providing a more clear and precise transmission or communication of emotions. In a film, the relation of the actor and the public is indirect; it is through an image, so films have less capability to transmit emotions than live theatre performances.

The filmed image needs to overcome this disadvantage with respect to live theatre by using methods that will allow the capture of emotions in the images as precisely as possible. On the other hand film has the advantage of keeping the final result of the creative process permanently, and can therefore be seen and re-seen over and over again.

The filmed image is equivalent for *Alba Emoting* to a scientific experiment in the laboratory in the sense that the scientific experiment requires measurements and repetitions in order to be valid. The filmed image is definite and can be seen, and responses to it measured qualitatively and quantitatively, as often as needed. This makes possible quantifying the observers' judgments that, as has been said, must be considered as scientifically valid.

The particular characteristics of the filmed image gave me the idea of presenting my work in a film that could illustrate what the written text could not communicate. I did not want to produce a classical documentary as I have always liked to build bridges between science and art.

I have always admired Pedro Sándor's original and creative style of filming and directing actors both in films and in the theatre. His essential role in the development of *Alba Emoting*, my desire to present my work with emotions in artistic images, and his powerful creative stamina, resulted in our great adventure of producing three films which constitute the *Alba Emoting* trilogy.

During the entire process in which I *actively participated*, I also had very special personal satisfaction since, because of his particular outlook on life and way of filming, he not only succeeded in transmitting the research and method artistically, but my soul and persona as well.

> In the autumn of 1990, we went for two weeks to the mountain area near Granada, Andalusia (Spain) staying in a small village lost in the Alpujarras, over the Costa del Sol. We took with us a common Sony camera, a small music recorder and a series of videos Pedro had filmed during different *Alba Emoting* workshops. The central structure of the film was built around a "conference" on the subject I improvised to the air and wind outside the village, walking around a stony platform while the camera followed me recording what I said in one continuous long shot. With this sequence as the core of the film, with interspersed extracts taken from previous *Alba Emoting* workshops, sounds of flamenco wails recorded from a local TV station, and a selection of operatic arias I had recorded, Pedro created a very original film. (See the script in Appendix II)

We named this film *Alba Emoting*. The other two films of the trilogy were named *My Way* and *Konstanz, Constancy* respectively. The films aimed to present the Emotional Effector Patterns and the use of the method in a structured, illustrative and attractive way, combining a scientific style of communication, with a certain poetic magic. I presented the film entitled *My Way* at a conference of the ISRE (*International Society for Research on Emotions*) of which I am a member.

Later on we did a totally different film, which is the above mentioned *Alba Emoting*. It illustrates the process of emotional induction, very vividly; including elements impossible to transmit in a written description. For instance one can see very clearly how as the actor follows the instructions in a particular way, his breathing and facial expression begin to change, and all the other body and gestural elements that organically correspond to the emotion induced by the special breath, begin to settle in. I myself am the main actress in the film.

When I showed the film at the Conference mentioned above, some of my colleagues, scientists and psychologists, found it to be very irreverent to present such precise and interesting data in a film intermingled with operas, masks, stones and Andalusian wails. They said that style of presentation detracted from the seriousness of my work.

Again the sacred territorialities. I have shown this film for over twenty years to many people of different nationalities, ages, professions and social conditions, and it always has a strong impact. Some theatre people have also had indignant reactions saying that it was an offense to their profession that I dared to act in the film, being a "scientist."

This was again, for me, a mission accomplished!

The film generates different reactions but its dramatic tension always grabs the attention of the spectator. It provokes discussion by presenting the subject in all its complexity, subtlety and even ethical dimensions. It can communicate in one second of lasting images a style of thinking and a particular perception of the subject in a clear, precise and artistic way.

The Chilean actress Isabel Santelices, who was trained in the method, wrote the following after watching the film:

> *"There is an image that stayed with me: it is when that mysterious woman (that is Susana) takes off her glove. And with a quick provocative gesture throws it into the air. It was like when Dumas' Musketeer takes off his glove and slaps someone's face with it. The image gives a slap to those who watch, independent of whether they agree or not with the method, because it obliges the spectator to wake up, think, to question many things. The film, undoubtedly, leaves you with a sensation. It provokes emotions. Some left in anger because they had been submitted to such provocative images, that they thought they had been submitted to a joke, or a trick. Others left in a happy mood, appreciating* what they had seen and felt, **but no one left indifferent**.*"*

In these times of quick images, clips, virtual realities, wonderful achievements obtained with sophisticated technologies, it is incredible that a film that was practically edited as it was shot, at no cost, with an everyday camera, done by two people collaborating with the best of their respective capabilities, can break barriers, open new horizons and bring joy.

I have used this film in a very special way: I always show it myself; **no copies circulate**; and I do so only to share my work and to provoke and motivate conversations and debates of any kind. Once I even showed it on a gigantic screen in an international festival of scientific films, in Paris, on the Eiffel Tower. I have never wanted to release it commercially.

> *Life must be lived*
> *In such a way*
> *That it remains alive*
> *In death.*

Finally *Konstanz, Constancy* is a film that shows the story of a mother-daughter relationship (my daughter Alejandra and myself) in a respectful confrontation of our two different worlds using the ***Alba Emoting*** method. It was filmed in three days in Konstanz, Germany in a small apartment and near the lake. Pedro Sándor, again camera in hand, filmed us two women: intermingled legs, a yellow dress, mirrors, Buñuel, surrealistic images, soft waves by the lake, interiors, exteriors, silence, boleros, German songs, brief discussions, music from Peter Brook's version of Bizet's Carmen, the Emotional Effector Patterns. The intimate atmosphere of the film reflects very well the emotional flow in human relations, in this case between mother and daughter.

The entire process of this filming with ***Alba Emoting*** as a background theme and starting point was very therapeutic and clarifying for the lives of these two women. To see the film, both for us who participated in it, as well as for the outside spectator who does not know the situation, evokes images, memories and reflections that help us to better understand our own emotions and those of others.

> *Primero es un albor trémulo y vago*
> *rayo de inquieta luz que corta el mar;*
> *luego chispea y crece y se dilata*
> *en ardiente explosión de claridad.*
> *La brilladora luz es la alegría;*
> *la tenebrosa sombra es el pesar:*
> *¡Ay!, en la oscura noche de mi alma,*
> *¿cuando amanecerá?*

At the beginning it is the dawn's trembling
vague ray of restless light that cuts the sea
and then glitters, grows, and dilates
in an ardent explosion of clarity.
The bright light is the joy.
The sinister shadow is the sorrow.
OH! In the dark night of my soul,
When will the day break?

(Rima LXII, de Gustavo Adolfo Bécquer)

# III. OPENING TO OTHER DOMAINS OF ACTION

If we are aware of the power of a glance, the strength of a gesture, the impact of a sigh, and the subtlety of a particular facial expression, we can understand that mastering a rigorous methodology based on the correct reproduction of concrete physical actions will allow us to express more clearly what we really feel. Only then will our emotional expressions generate the expected response or the appropriate emotional reaction in the observer (spectator, public, conversation partner).

In the same way that the method is applied in the fields of science, theatre and filming, **Alba Emoting** can be very useful in many other areas of human activity. There is a large new world open for exploration.

Here, briefly, are three experiences that illustrate possible applications the method can offer, one which I developed personally in the area of publicity, another that is an example of its use in organizational development, and finally an application in the field of psychotherapy.

## PUBLICITY

There is a huge potential for utilizing a method that allows the trained user to express and modulate precise emotional messages and correctly communicate them, without distortions or ambiguities and in a fast and efficient way.

> Some years ago in France I was invited to participate in an international meeting organized by consultants for television advertising. The idea was to apply scientific knowledge for a better understanding of consumer behavior. It was attended by a wide variety of academic specialists in areas such as paralinguistic, neurophysiology, and TV

advertisement, and the debate was conducted by one of the most well-known anchormen of French TV. The subject that year was "*The art of the subliminal or hidden message.*"

After listening to my presentation, illustrated with images from the **Alba Emoting** film, the head of an important advertisement agency approached me and said that he was greatly impressed by the power of the emotional messages that emerged from the reproduced Emotional Effector Patterns.

A few days later, he contacted me and asked me to advise him in his development of a campaign to advertise a new shaving product for a well-known cosmetics company. The aim was to choose, under the most objective criteria possible, the photo of a male that would best communicate a message of "satisfaction, seduction, and complicity."

The set of photos, that had already been taken, showed shots of the face of a man who was supposed to transmit these emotional states. This was the first time that in my capacity as an "expert" in emotional expression, I could apply our scientific findings for a commercial ad. So, with my research team, we analyzed over 100 photographs in my laboratory searching in the photos for the presence of the expressive pattern that would best transmit the chosen emotions the sponsors wanted in the final poster. We analyzed the direction of the gaze, the gestures of the hands, the head orientation, in fact all the parameters that corresponded to the desired emotions. The photo we finally selected for the best emotional expressiveness resulted in the client's complete satisfaction.

Sometime later, a note appeared in *Creation Magazine*, which specialized in advertisement, in which the director of the agency expressed the importance of being able to confirm intuitive judgments with scientific data, since both approaches had been closely in agreement.

It is very satisfying for any researcher to be able to confirm experimental data obtained in laboratory situations —which are generally concerned with basic research and therefore remain in the academic domain—, and to see how the data can be applied in life.

Later on, a young student from the *Institut Supérieur de Publicité et de Communication dans les Entreprises* in France, did a final paper for his degree in my laboratory with these results and a review on the concepts and practice of **Alba Emoting** as applied to the domain of advertisement, especially for ad campaigns that had strong emotional significance. The paper was entitled *Communiquer l'Émotion*.

The elements that are intentionally aimed at in an advertisement probably always serve one or more "purposes" and none of them must be ignored. But without doubt it is the emotional expressivity of the ad that has the most important advertising impact.

## ORGANIZATIONAL DEVELOPMENT

Since I had no personal experience in the world of organizations, I asked the entrepreneur and consultant Mauricio Gonzalez M. to write something about his experience in using **Alba Emoting** in his work. Here is a transcription of what he sent to me by mail:

> *"My recognition of and gratitude to Susana Bloch and her **Alba Emoting System** has two aspects:*
>
> *1. My eleven years of experience as an entrepreneur with my Ti 5 company, whose goal was to generate spaces for meeting people through dancing, and*
>
> *2. My work of the ten years, which aims to recover the human soul in organizations.*
>
> *I still recall when I met with Susana in 1996 in a basic workshop which she conducted in which she asked us students at the end to sign a document in which we promised not to use her method. I did not sign it... which was good because my refusal opened the door to dialogue, discussion and the beginning of a prolific friendship with Susana, the psychologist, the artist, and with the overwhelming energy of her humanity.*
>
> *With respect to the Ti-5, the benefits for my team of twenty one teachers were basically two. On the one hand it was the knowledge of the emotional patterns that were behind the dances we were working with. That understanding gave us a clarity and insight to be conscious of what we were inducing with the different music and movements we were teaching, and therefore become much more lucid and effective in our daily activities. The second benefit was the STEP-OUT... essential for our teachers who are continuously exposed to their emotions when directing human groups in movements triggered by the dances. The ability to do the step-out exercises at the end of each class opened a place of great benefit and spiritual balance to my team.*
>
> *Shortly after I began with the Ti-5 project, I was solicited by different organizations to help engender creative, collaborative, trustful and joyful moods*

*inside the companies through programs of intensive weekends or seminars of longer duration. And even though the subjects were the usual ones —team work, leadership, entrepreneurial abilities, innovation and creativity in a changing world, and attitudes of service— in my opinion the big problem is that in our successful mechanistic and technological modern world (including the organizational one), a big shadow accompanies each apparent success, and that is the loss of our sense of humanity in our daily lives.*

*I have been lucky to work in Chile, Argentina, Venezuela, and Mexico with small, medium, large, and multinational companies of production and of service, both public and private at all levels: with workers, employees, executives, directors, and operators.*

*The direct physical contact with the basic emotions provided by the* **Alba Emoting** *system has been for me essential in the openness that the participants in our courses have been able to achieve, in terms of transcending the emotional restraints of modernity. This, together with a lucid, playful atmosphere, free movements plus blessed language, can, in my opinion, accelerate learning at a surprising rate.*

***Alba Emoting**, physical in its practice, scientific in its basis and amazing in its emotional effectiveness, is definitely a strong support for the flourishing of my own work in Playful Learning in Movement. We have faced the companies' needs with a playful approach that facilitates human encounters in the most natural learning pyramid: first the physical, then the emotional, and finally the level of reasoning and language.*

*In this sense the application of the* **Alba Emoting** *system has been fundamental and powerful in my work with organizations, since it has allowed me to intervene physically in the emotional being of the participants of our programs, thus helping them avoid big conflicts.*

*In all our programs with organizations:*

> *The play is the form*
> *To dance, to breathe and to talk is the context*
> *Silence is the transcendence.*

***Alba Emoting*** *is immersed in the heart of our work.*
> *What more do we need?"*

(Mauricio Gonzalez M.)

Nowadays it is common in all kinds of organizations (families, syndicates, political groups, business, schools, sports, and so on among many others) to deal with themes such as group spirit, team-work, leadership, creativity, communication, validating humanity, decency and ethics. Emotions are crucial in dealing with all such subjects. ***Alba Emoting*** has proved to be most relevant as an important method for working with them. ***Alba Emoting*** provides basic support for any technique, method or system that needs to work with emotions in organizational development.

For example, if someone needs to express a feeling of comradeship or of tenderness in a meeting with colleagues, the tender pattern can be used. It can also be very effective to work with the anger pattern when there is a need to express or to ask for something assertively, or to learn how to step out of a sad mood before presiding at an important meeting.

## PSYCHOTHERAPY

A very important area for application of the method is in psychotherapy. The therapist who knows and masters the method has a great tool to help, for example, people who have emotional blocks or who cannot express certain emotions adequately, or people who think they are expressing a particular emotion when in fact they express and convey quite the opposite. It also helps people who are confused with what they are feeling, or who are unaware of having mixed feelings which they cannot differentiate.

For example, when one lives through the dissolution of love, what is the emotion one is really feeling? Is it sadness, anger, jealousy, or fear of being left alone? Each one of these emotional states has very different physical and subjective connotations. The ***Alba Emoting*** method allows a person suffering because of a failed love affair to become aware of the dynamics of the process in order to make appropriate distinctions among the various mixed feelings experienced, so as to be able to use specific exercises that will help form direct contact with truly felt emotions.

One can certainly attain different emotional states by singing, dancing or recalling a particular situation, but the emotions that may emerge in such cases will vary according to the moment, the particular memory evoked, or the situation the person is placed in at that precise moment. This is exactly what happens in daily life and even more so in situations specially created to provoke such effects.

The emotion elicited with their execution of a specific Emotional Pattern emerges as if pointed at by a laser beam, so to speak, that points directly to one particular emotion which then simply appears.

There are patients who, for instance, cannot express anger or who do not realize what anxiety really is, and therefore may spend long periods of time in therapy trying to analyze what is happening to them, talking about it, trying to verbalize what seems very confusing. With **Alba Emoting**, if the therapist teaches the patient a precise breathing pattern, in only a few minutes the patient may directly experience first the physical and then the emotional feeling of what really is anger, sadness or fear. The emotion will emerge immediately and is real, direct, pure, and alive.

>One of my then students in **Alba Emoting**, Juan Pablo Kalawski, got his Master's degree in Psychology at the Universidad Central, Chile, by applying the method to a group of patients who were in therapy. His thesis was based on the working hypothesis that the use of the method would produce, among other effects, a rise in the clients' levels of "experiencing."

>Kalawski observed the difficulty that one of his "clients" had in connecting with his feelings and the vagueness with which he described his anxieties. Suspecting the presence of a hidden primary emotion, (probably the true repressed emotion) he taught him to do the sadness pattern and after a good Step-Out, asked him what he had felt, to which the patient answered with great assuredness, that in fact he had felt a deep sadness.

>In another session doing the anger pattern helped this patient to really experience full anger without mixing it with fear. This allowed him later to feel more secure in a real life situation in which anger was the appropriate reaction.

The method thus becomes an extremely useful intervention in the dynamics of therapy, as it increases the level, precision and quality of the patient's "experiencing" and at the same time refines and tunes the distinctions made among the different emotional states. I recently asked Kalawski —who has by now many years of professional experience with the method— to write a reflection on the subject to include in this chapter. He sent me the following from the United States where he is presently living:

>*"We psychotherapists always work with emotions. However, there are diverse opinions as to how to approach them. Some of us believe that emotions should be actively stimulated in the therapy process. Other therapists think this is not a good idea. Such a point of view is quite legitimate. Let us suppose as an example that a person is constantly criticizing his or her partner. There is*

*a belief that "emotions should be let out," based on the assumption that the person's anger would disappear once the emotion has been "let out." Psychologists, however, know that the mere exteriorization of a problematic emotion does not end it and can, on the contrary, increase it.*

*Some therapists, therefore, believe that it is better to emphasize changes in behavior, and especially in the client's thinking. The majority of therapists, though, at least talk about emotions. Even within this rather restricted perspective,* **Alba Emoting** *is useful for therapists, since it helps them recognize their client's various emotions, and consequently better understand their difficulties.*

*I am convinced of the method's usefulness for training perceptions. For instance if one looks at an X-ray, one can hardly distinguish the differences within a group of bones. Good radiologists, however, can see exactly where the problem is. In the same way* **Alba Emoting** *helps develop the ability to perceive emotions accurately, both in oneself as well as in others. When I meet with my colleagues to observe videos of therapy sessions, I can help them recognize their clients' emotions by observing how they move and how they breathe.*

**Alba Emoting** *is a method that activates emotions, and this is its most specific contribution for therapy. Coming back to the example of the person continually criticizing his or her partner, it is clear that the person is "caught" in one emotion, in this case anger. As I already said, simply ventilating this anger will not finish it. What I do as a therapist in such a case is to stimulate other emotions that are present to a certain degree but are not acknowledged, for example sadness or fear. This procedure helps clients widen their perspectives.*

*All basic emotions are potentially adaptive but some people have blocked their capacity to experience certain emotions. In such cases* **Alba Emoting** *can be very useful. The experience of an emotion that one has not experienced in a long time or never in a particular context can open a whole world of possibilities. Take, for instance, the case of tenderness, an emotion that has been marginalized in our patriarchal culture. At present I am investigating this emotion more deeply, since it has also been marginalized from psychological research.*

*Very often people avoid emotions that they believe are negative. For example trying to repress sadness can lead to expressing anger, which results in pushing others away. The "Step-Out" technique is not repression, but rather a means of returning to a calm state. This technique also has the advantage of being simple and secure, requiring no major training.*

*We human beings come into this world with a system that generates emotions that most of the time are adaptive.* **Alba Emoting** *allows us to recognize these emotions, modulate their intensity, and keep us from getting distracted* *by secondary emotions. Human beings need both excitation and calmness. The **Alba Emoting** method allows us to evoke both states."*

Though I am a psychologist myself I have not specialized in therapy. I am convinced, however, that therapists with any methodological approach can apply **Alba Emoting** in their work, since once the basic emotion – which is necessarily present behind any problem or conflict– has been clearly, physically perceived and therefore experienced, it is possible to approach the causes of the conflict and eventually solve it.

In the various workshops that I have conducted with different people, I have often found that without having intended it, the mere reproduction of an emotional breathing pattern, which can be instructed and experienced on the spot, will for some participants act as true therapy, clarifying underlying psychological problems or conflicts they may have.

# FINAL COMMENTS

In the prologue of this book, Pedro Sándor says very appropriately that **"For big evils, great remedies."**

I fully agree with him.

Looking back in time, one could say that when human beings lived more in contact with their ecological niche, in stable, familiar surroundings, in small communities near nature, basic emotions were a natural part of their lives. But in the present time, we spend most of our lives in contact with machines (computers, television, electronic music, etc.) all of which are robotic, don't really communicate, and have no emotions. Soon we become like them. Our daily life transforms us into automatons.

In our highly technological society it becomes an urgent, vital need to recover our truly human dimension –the ability to communicate authentically– which cannot exist without the capacity for feeling.

How can we recover our capacity for feeling and relating emotionally with each other?

The discovery of *Alba Emoting* appears precisely at the moment when it is needed for recovering the legitimacy of our emotional dimension, and especially of those more atavistic and adaptive emotions that connect us with the real world and open our possibilities for transcending our present limited emotional behavior. And it is a simple method that allows us to connect instantly and unequivocally with basic emotions, starting physically, in a non-psychological, non-cathartic and scientifically validated way.

*Alba Emoting*, being a precise physical system –**breathing for emoting**– is at the basis of any endeavor that deals with problems of any kind, physical, intellectual and/or, of course, emotional, since emotions play an essential role in the body-mind connection. It is amazing to realize how useful this system can be in so many areas of activities. Each of you who reads this book may develop, from your own interests and specializations, new applications. The road is new, promising, and wide open.

Nowadays more than ever, the role of emotional networking is recognized as essential in any organization, since the success or failure of any human group activity will depend on the effectiveness of those networks, which in turn depend upon good emotional communication. This is so true that it is even said that the relevance of the intelligence quotient concept (IQ) will be replaced by that of emotional intelligence (EI), **as a primary factor needed to understand the mechanisms of human functioning in all areas of activities.**

Let us review the fundamental components of the Emotional Intelligence concept:

- The capacity of being conscious of one's own emotions.
- The ability to handle moods.
- The capacity for self-motivation (being optimistic),
- The capacity for recognizing emotions in others (empathy),
- The social abilities needed to persuade, organize and direct.

***Alba Emoting*** **is in fact indispensable in developing emotional intelligence, as it proposes a direct, practical, physical method that develops precisely the above mentioned abilities needed for good emotional mastery.**

Expanding the concept of E.I. even more, today one speaks of the importance of managing the moods of a sports team, of an entire country and so on.

In short, *Alba Emoting* is a powerful tool to develop emotional mastery, and to facilitate communication for any human being, independent of race, cultural values or gender. The system is by definition universal, biological, non-psychological, culture-free and independent of the past history and memories of the individual who uses it.

I want to express this now more clearly by saying that:

**The Emotional Effector Patterns are Universal, Non-Psychological, Non-Historical, Non-Cultural. They are Biologically Absolute.**

In the midst of a native untouched forest, in the most southern part of Latin America, I embrace an "alerce," a sequoia-like tree native to Chile, pure, austere, four thousand years old, thirty meters high. There one is naked, in contact with our most atavistic, non-contaminated emotions. No neurosis is possible. The relation between the basic emotions and the million year old forest, between the basic emotions and the "natural nature of things" then becomes evident.

**Besides its technical and practical utility, the method engenders a different outlook on the vast subject of emotions. It recovers the legitimacy of the basic emotions, suppressing value judgments, such as "bad" or "good"; it fully recognizes their biological basis, their intrinsic adaptability, their essential role in everyday life and their use in understanding mixed emotions, moods and higher emotions (e.g. sublimity).**

Some years ago we did an experiment with an actress who was well-trained in the method. I asked her —we were under conditions of absolute trust— to reproduce the pattern of sadness for as long as possible. The exercise lasted for sixteen minutes and the entire process was filmed. The actress began the exercise very technically as usual, but very soon she entered into true sadness and began to weep, but she always kept her concentration on the instructed exercise. The weeping intensified, but at no time did she lose control or become hysterical. She maintained the intentional breathing rhythm, entering at the same time into her own emotions. At the end she dropped to the floor from sheer physical exhaustion and ended the exercise by her own decision. She immediately proceeded with the Step-Out, which in this case lasted longer and was performed more systematically than is usual. When she finally calmed down, I asked her what had happened; if she had had images; and what in fact she had experienced. She said it had been like "all the pain in the world" a kind of *Weltschmertz* with feelings of great compassion for and understanding of all suffering human beings. Though she had also evoked some memories of personal painful moments of her life, what had been her dominant feeling was this very real compassion for the suffering humanity.

From the many different experiences I myself have had with the method, initially in the domain of theatre and later in different areas such as psychotherapy, organizational development, advertisement and others, it is evident that another important and large area of application is the possibility of working with mixed and with higher emotions. These are the emotions that mostly permeate our daily psychologically complex world. *Alba Emoting* is also needed in spaces of "emotional silence." It is precisely in these spaces that the Step-Out technique plays an essential role similar to the one we have seen used as a cooling-down procedure for the theatre. It provides a powerful technique that allows us to stop the whirlwind of emotions evoked by present life situations when they overwhelm us.

Let me stress once more that when we have directly experienced the six basic emotions and have had a glimpse of the complex mixed emotions and have learned how to get out of them, I believe that only then are we able to live in harmony, with good quality-of-life. We can then be at peace with our whole complex and wonderful psychological world even with all the mixed emotion that dominates our daily lives.

In conclusion, we must not forget that it is precisely due to its intrinsic power and efficacy that the method may become dangerous in irresponsible hands. The benefits of the method will largely depend on the style of teaching and of the maturity, sensibility and human qualities of both teachers and learners.

The power of being able to evoke emotions by simply changing one's breathing pattern is like having the reins of a wild horse in one's hands; a horse that must be guided by a professional rider, a rider who is full of humanity, who has great spiritual integrity and is capable of adapting the guidelines of the method creatively, but always ethically. If someone with dark intentions holds the reins, the method may turn into something harmful, so that the horse, to continue the analogy, may bolt and hurt the rider.

To teach this method according to these requirements is not a job for everyone; one needs systematic training. Therefore I am forming a solid, well-trained team so that the method will be taught and disseminated by teachers who, with their own styles, will nevertheless always keep the essential quality that the work with *Alba Emoting* has and, hopefully, will always continue to have.

In daily life, when there is a strong emotion, we get submerged in it. We lose control. It is as if a huge ocean wave smashes over us and knocks us down. We are at the mercy of that powerful wave.

Using *Alba Emoting* does not mean we will not live our daily emotions intensely; on the contrary, we will acquire a greater capacity to experience them fully. The method allows us to surf creatively on the waves of emotions, without getting tumbled and bruised by them.

I write while listening to the soft sound of the rain on the thatched roof of my house near the ocean. The fire sparkles on the hearth. I prepare myself a cup of herbal tea. I am alone, but surrounded by nature. The wooden room is softly illuminated. I feel well, balanced, in harmony with my surroundings.

*Yo no quiero la gloria ni la paz,*
*a mí sólo me toca la magia*

I don't want glory nor peace
Only let magic touch me

*(Mujeres de Ojos Grandes)*
(From *Women with Big Eyes* by Angeles Mastretta)

# FINAL WORDS OF THE AUTHOR
# TO THIS SECOND REVISED EDITION

For more than thirty years my life has been strongly linked with **Alba Emoting**. This powerful connection has allowed me and others to connect more deeply and vitally with the Magic of Living.

This is specially reflected in the words of Elizabeth Townsend and Patricia Angelin who impelled me to publish this Second Edition. I wish to thank them here for their unfailing commitment to make it possible.

> *For eighteen months we worked by telephone and mainly through Skype, since they both live in different cities in the United States of North America, and I live in Santiago, Chile, South America.*
>
> *Our interactions, in spite of such distance, were so vivid, rich and creative, that most of the time I had the feeling that we three were sitting in my living room here in Santiago.*

I will place here below a testimony of the experience Elizabeth and Patricia have lived with **Alba Emoting**, because their own words transmit very well the deep, strong and sophisticated engagement both have with **Alba Emoting**.

# ELIZABETH ANN TOWNSEND

My first exposure to **Alba Emoting** was in 2001 when my longtime dear friend and **Alba Emoting** instructor, Professor Roxane Rix, taught me the Joy Effector Pattern to assist me in preparing for an audition. I had been a professional actress for 20 years at the time and had studied many acting techniques from professionals in New York City. But, from the first moment in my cottage with Roxane's assistance when I began to experience joy growing in me from even just the breath aspect of the Joy Effector Pattern, I knew I had found at last what I was looking for in a technique for accessing organic emotion. I have never looked back.

In the ensuing 11 years, I have studied **Alba Emoting** in the United States and, in 2011, I had the wonderful good fortune to get to know personally and study directly with Dr. Susana Bloch in Chile. In every role that I have played and will play, **Alba Emoting** is the cornerstone of my character's emotional life and is the emotional melody I follow throughout the journey of the play or film. I have to say, that all the techniques in the world that could lead you to understand your character and the world they live in, **Alba Emoting** is the only system I have found that consistently provides me with the emotional life every time I need it, when I need it, and how I need it.

During a rehearsal as Madame from Jean Genet's play, *The Maids*, when my character discovers her utter love and total grief over the imprisonment of her lover, I was exploring the moment by mixing the Effector Patterns of Joy, Erotic Love, and Sadness. When the scene was over and it was time for a break, I released the patterns and laughed. It had been so much fun! The director who was from Poland was completely astonished at the quickness of my return to myself! He was convinced that it should have taken me at least a few minutes to recover! He had been completely drawn in by my emotional state to then discover that it had been only *art?!* "No," I said! "It is Alba Emoting!" He teased me but I could see he felt he had witnessed a magical moment of pure, unrepeatable inspiration, which of course he had, except that I had **Alba Emoting** and would take the journey again.

I was particularly grateful for **Alba Emoting** during the performances of Garcia Lorca's *Blood Wedding* in which I played the Mother. The director's concept was to have me sitting with my back to the audience as people arrived to take their seats. Along with me on stage was a wonderful guitarist playing flamenco music. I had discovered during rehearsals that Mother is steeped in the mixed emotions of Fear, Anger, and Sadness throughout the play, and all three had to be alive in my body at differing levels from the moment I took my seat on stage with my back to the audience 15 minutes before the play would actually begin. The mixed emotions radiated from my body, infecting the atmosphere of the space. When the lights came up on the set, the audience was already aware on a visceral level that the circumstances about to unfold were full of my character's dread.

As the demise of my son progresses to its seemingly preordained and devastating conclusion and consequently the utter despair that I, as an actress, was required to experience and channel every performance, my emotional commitment could have varied night to night if the necessary emotional state had depended on my dredging up painful emotions that my psyche may not want to, or even could, induce every time. But, with **Alba Emoting**, I had access to what I needed every moment along the way on that desolating journey. And I, as an actress, suffered much less than I would have if I did not have this essential tool and the ability to Step-Out when it was over. **Alba Emoting** gave me the courage to step back into Mother the following day, knowing that I would always be safe in my technique.

Saint Louis, Missouri's Washington University Medical School has a Standardized Patient Program which provides medical students with the experience of asking the right questions that will lead to accurate diagnosis as well as give them the opportunity to practice one-on-one communication with patients in a low risk situation. This is done with actors standing in as real patients. I was hired to play a woman with Chronic Obstructive Pulmonary Disorder (COPD), brought on by 30 years of smoking 2 packs of cigarettes per day. My instructions were to be sad and tearful during each session that lasted 30 minutes with 13 individual medical students of Pharmacology over the period of 8 hours. That meant 6 1/2 hours of often nearly back to back sessions of calling up sadness and tears! In the 5 minutes or so between students, I would drop the Sadness Pattern to take a brief break before beginning it again only moments before the next student knocked on the door to enter.

The Sadness Effector Pattern created the atmosphere of sadness and remorse in me and in the room for every student so that they could have the experience of relating with compassion to a patient as a whole being and not just someone with a physical problem to solve. These young medical students will be going out into the real world and treating us in the not too distant future. ***Alba Emoting*** helped me give them the opportunity to tune into a patient as a person and what the person is feeling, to treat a person, not just an illness. I could not have effectively given them this experience consistently without extreme emotional exhaustion, if at all, had I not been using ***Alba Emoting***.

I forever owe a debt of gratitude to Susana Bloch and her curiosity and commitment to the development of ***Alba Emoting***. I strongly encouraged her to publish this second edition of her book, *The Alba Of Emotions*, in order to reach a broader audience in the English speaking world, and more importantly, so that those who read it will have the opportunity to begin their own exploration of this life changing technique.

Elizabeth Ann Townsend<br>
Saint Louis, Missouri, USA

# PATRICIA ANGELIN

My involvement with **Alba Emoting** began over two decades ago when I walked into a too-small hotel conference room in the venerable Palmer House hotel in Chicago. Tired, and fresh off a plane from an acting job in Europe, I knew nothing about Dr. Susana Bloch or **Alba Emoting**. *Nada.* Nothing at all. All I remember about the blurb in the prospectus that propelled me into that room was the promise of *Neutrality*. Wow. The Holy Grail. An emotionally neutral state on demand is beyond price, particularly to an actor, who needs to function as an "athlete of the emotions!"

So…although I was twelve minutes late for the session I crashed the party, as it were. Upon entering I saw university professors along three walls, crushed together three-deep. They were observing several people lying supine on the floor doing some kind of exercise, breathing… while a lithe European-looking Lady with a vibrant elemental presence moved among them orchestrating…what? A gentleman shoved over to make room for me. I sat.

The Lady beckoned me forward. I was astonished, and looked around to see if it was really me to whom she gestured. She nodded, put a finger to her lips, and then toward the floor. There was no possibility of refusing this woman. After removing my hat, I lay on my back in the last piece of available floor-space… and Susana Bloch proceeded to change my life.

I certainly did not know at the time, (nor could Susana) that I was a scientifically sought-after "naïve subject"—all I knew then was that I would focus fully and respond to the technical instructions of an acting exercise….

Susana spoke quietly into my ear, "Please breathe this way…. I shall layer instructions upon this breath. Please continue the breathing." She returned to me perhaps five times, moving my limbs, adjusting my head, giving muscular tension commands, instructing me on the opening of my eyes, as I continued to concentrate solely on that special breathing. Finally, this magic Personage said, "Now, if possible, un-focus your eyes." I managed it, and… Zap… Pow… Zowee! I was in full-blown, out-of-nowhere (as it seemed to me) sexual arousal. Good grief. The feeling was in my whole body. 'All-systems-go.' And, as I suddenly became uncomfortably aware, I was in front of a roomful of judgmental strangers. *What is this?!*

Just as I was feeling a bit overwhelmed by what I was observing in my body—unconnected to any normal external or psychological stimuli—thank goodness Susana saved my no-longer-maiden blushes. She directed us to rise from the floor and taught her revolutionary Step-Out procedure. The Step-Out turned off my "turn-on" like a water faucet. And that was the real miracle; I was Neutral. Hosanna, Susana! Alleluia.

The experience of that single exercise was so specific, so intense, and so authentic, that to this day, by emotional memory, I would be able to call it up even without using ***Alba Emoting***. My "emotional induction" was recorded and entered into Dr. Bloch's scientific literature. I cancelled my other engagements and went directly to an intensive training at Susana's invitation… and that was the beginning of my continuing odyssey with ***Alba Emoting***.

As my colleague, Elizabeth Townsend, has shared with us in regard to *mixed* emotions (which is one of the chief uses onstage and screen), ***Alba Emoting*** has many uses once it is mastered. First and foremost it opens the artist's creative instrument like nothing else, even very early on.

I will share with you an anecdote about one specific application of the method to *unmixed* emotion.

I had been working with Susana on ***Alba Emoting*** as frequently as our schedules allowed for nearly a decade at the time, but it was work that I had largely kept to myself. I knew it was powerful, but was about to discover *how* powerful its impact was on an audience in its pure form.

I had a callback audition for a large committee of a governmental Council of the Arts for whom I had been asked to perform a single monologue. I decided to use the audition completely for my own actor process. Having made that decision, I thought, "Okay, how can I make this creatively fun for myself?" "I know, I'll put ***Alba Emoting*** to a final test!"

I decided that I'd pick only one of the six core emotions out of a hat; I drew "Anger." Then I decided to 'up the ante,' and added to my self-challenge by making it more difficult: not only would I breathe Anger, I would do it without speaking. And not only without speaking, but *also* with my back to the audience… *and* without moving! **Alba Emoting** had been challenged indeed.

I walked into the large audition ballroom, cordially greeted the panel, and set a chair center-stage. I turned my back to them with my left hand casually draped over the chair-back, and began to breathe a very low-intensity level Anger Pattern, my body to all appearances perfectly still. The room quieted instantly. As I continued that simple breath, the tension in the room began to become palpable. The audience was so concentrated that I could feel their attention become more and more lazar-focused on me. My authentically felt Anger was pulling them in. I could keep their attention as long as I chose. Power, indeed, and I hadn't even "done" anything. Finally, after perhaps a minute and a half of this breathing—an eternity onstage—I decided, from within the Anger Pattern, "Oh, come on, Pat, give 'em a little something." At that point all my thoughts had Anger in them. So I deigned to lift my little finger from that chair-back. A woman gasped. I spoke—responding in the moment to her response. 'Acting is Reacting' as the saying goes. My voice was *sotto voce*, and so intensely intimate that I could feel them each and all lean in. It was as though each audience member was the only person to whom I spoke. Then I turned and continued the monologue. **Alba Emoting** filled the whole room…my character filled the whole room. It was real. It was pure. It was electric.

There is nothing more powerful than unadulterated, authentic human emotion. Nothing.

Now, as I have had **Alba Emoting** all these years as a personal tool, I have the added bounty of sharing this work as a Teacher of **Alba Emoting** in New York and internationally. This not only benefits the craft of actors, but is also for the well being of any person who desires to engage in this work for the development of the Self.

One evening, as I prepared to speak to Susana about this book, I suddenly had a vision. Here is what I shared with my dear mentor and friend when we spoke:

> I was *there* with you at your Cachagua hearthside, watching you as you wrote. Then, just as suddenly, I was at the tiny inlet of the Pacific down the cliff from your retreat… I was standing in Las Cujas thigh-deep, as an overwhelming wave approached me. I felt the primal fear

of the power of the world's greatest Ocean—I would be engulfed, pulled out to sea and drown!—in the next instant, that warm, salty wave washed completely over my body. It embraced me, and I was given to understand in that moment that… it had contained and I had been given… *all the emotions*.

Real magic, with big open eyes.

Patricia Angelin
New York, New York

# EPILOGUE

And finally, I, Susana Bloch, say goodbye to my book, sustained by a poem Pedro Sándor wrote '*clamus correnti*' (as the pen runs) on a windy morning in April 2009.

### SILENCIO

*Viví lo Absoluto*
*Como Quise*
*Soplando Infinitos*
*Recogiendo Flores*
*Bebiendo el Nectar*
*De la Gran*
*Soledad Final.*

### SILENCE

I lived the Absolute
As I Desired
Collecting Flowers
Blowing Infinities
Drinking the Nectar
of the Great
Final Solitude.

Susana Bloch Arendt
Santiago, Chile

# APPENDIX I*

## Specific respiratory patterns distinguish among human basic emotions

Susana Bloch, Madeleine Lemeignan, y Nancy Aguilera T.
Institut des Neurosciences – CNRS, Laboratoire de Neurochimie-Anatomie. Université Pierre et Marie Curie, 9, quai Saint-Bernard, 75005 Paris, France. (Accepted 2 November 1990)

Key words: Emotional breathing: Respiratory parameter; Basic emotion; Emotional effector pattern; Emotional induction; Respiration; Emotion

Prototypical respiratory-facial-postural actions ('Emotional Effector patterns') related to six basic emotions had been extracted from an ensemble of physiological reactions present in subjects reliving intense emotional situations (Bloch & Santibañez, 1972). Subjects reproducing these actions could evoke the corresponding subjective experience, which suggested their use as an experimental model for generating controlled emotional states. The aim of the present study was to quantify the respiratory parameters which characterize the emotions of joy-laughter, sadness-crying, fear-anxiety, anger, erotic love and tenderness. Respiratory movements and facial/postural expressions were recorded from 36 young actors who had learned in previous workshops to express these emotions by reproducing the corresponding prototypical actions. A qualitative analysis of the recordings showed that as the emotional reproduction went along, both breathing and expression evolved from an initial 'robot-like' phase to a

---

* From International Journal of Psychophysiology, 11 (1991) 141-15; © 1991 Elsevier Science Publishers B.V. 0167-8760/91. PSYCHO 00345

NB: Readers who wish to view this scientific article as originally formatted in Journal publication are referred to www.elsevier.com, where the publisher gives free Open Access to the archives.

more natural stage in which spontaneous vocalizations and gestures appeared. This suggested a partial activation of the emotional network. The quantitative analysis of the respiratory movements for the fundamental cycles showed that for anger, erotic love and tenderness significant changes in amplitudes rate and duration of the 'expiratory pause' were the major elements of differentiation, while for sadness, joy and fear inspiratory over expiratory time ratios were the elements of differentiation. These last three emotions were further characterized by small amplitude/high rate saccadic respiratory movements superposed to different phases of the fundamental cycles. It is concluded that quantitatively well differentiated sets of respiratory changes characterize each of six basic emotions. The bottom-up experimental model for generating such emotions based on the joint activation of the respiratory-facial-postural systems and its relation to corresponding 'real-life' emotions is discussed.

## INTRODUCTION

The ensemble of characteristic respiratory, postural and facial changes arising during intense emotional states is what Bloch and Santibañez (1972) designated as the 'Emotional Effector patterns'. In their original study these authors recorded respiratory movements, muscular activity, heart rate, blood pressure, expressive features and subjective reports in normal subjects who were reliving intense emotional situations under deep hypnosis and in awake drama students who were asked to remember as vividly as possible emotionally charged life experiences. The most interesting outcome of these recordings was that during the emotional activation, together with the typical facial expressions, gestures and dynamic postures that the subjects adopted according to the type of emotion, specific changes in respiration occurred which were also distinctive for each emotional revival. Respiratory recordings as adapted from the original study are illustrated in Fig. 1 (a, b).

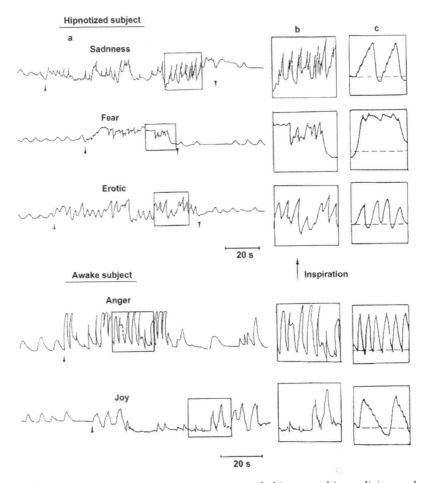

Fig. 1. (a) Changes of respiratory movements recorded in one subject reliving under deep hypnosis, personal emotional situations related to sadness, fear and erotic love (adapted from the original recordings, Bloch and Santibañez, 1972) and in two awake subjects during spontaneous episodes of anger and joy. Upward arrow tips: beginning of the emotional revival. Downward arrow tips: end of the hypnotic suggestion. For the awake subjects, duration of the spontaneous emotions have their own time course. (b) Respiratory movements present by the end of the emotional episodes, framed-in and enlarged. (e) Schematic drawings of the corresponding prototypical emotional breathing patterns (adapted from Santibañez & Bloch, 1986). Dashed lines give an indication of the lowest level of expiration that is attained during neutral non-emotional states.

From the complex viscero-muscular reactions which occurred during these intensely relived emotions, Bloch and Santibañez (1972) considered those which can be under voluntary control, i.e., the changes in respiratory movements, in facial expressions and in body posture. The authors extracted the most prominent features of these changes for six basic emotions: joy-laughter, sadness-crying, fear-anxiety, anger-agression, erotic love and tenderness (Santibañez & Bloch, 1986). The resulting prototypical respiratory-facial-postural configurations for each emotion are what they called Emotional Effector patterns. The respiratory prototypes are shown in Fig. 1c.

Since the emotional patterns are under voluntary control, the authors gave naive subjects general indications for reproducing them. Interestingly enough, they observed that the mere reproduction of the instructed actions could arouse in the performer the corresponding subjective experience (Bloch et al., 1987). Moreover, the emotional message was unequivocally transmitted since non-adverted observers correctly identified the emotion corresponding to each reproduction (Aguilera et al., 1989).

The property of driving other elements of an emotional system by reproducing an ensemble of well-defined prototypical somatic actions suggested the use of these Emotional Effector patterns as an experimental model for generating emotions in a controlled way (Bloch, 1989). Such a model is essentially different from the techniques most commonly employed such as presenting visual material containing strong emotional valence (e.g., Buck et al., 1974; Wagner et al., 1986), or giving instructions to recall, visualize or imagine particular emotional events (e.g., Lang et al., 1980; Schwartz et al., 1981; Fridlund et al., 1984; Smith et al., 1986). The reproduction of the Emotional Effector patterns has the advantage of using precise, objective and reproducible actions comprising the joint activation of three systems, respiratory, facial and postural.

The relation of each of these systems to specific emotions has so far been analyzed separately, the face being the one most thoroughly explored (see for example Izard, 1971; Ekman & Oster, 1979; Rinn, 1984). A smaller but increasing number of investigators have been dealing with the postural system (Ekman & Friesen, 1967; Mehrabian, 1968; Riskind, 1984; Kudoh & Matsumoto, 1985; Duclos et al., 1989; Sogon & Masutani, 1989). With respect to the respiratory system the great majority of investigations have been centered on the role of emotional states in respiratory and cardiovascular diseases (see reviews by Grossman, 1983 and Bass & Gardner,

1985a), on the relationship of respiratory and psychiatric disorders (Finesinger, 1944; Christie, 1935; Damas-Mora et al., 1976, 1982; Dudley & Pitts-Poarch, 1980; Rosser & Guz, 1981) and on the relation between breathing characteristics and dispositional or personality traits (Alexander & Saul, 1940; Christiansen, 1965; Shea et al., 1987). Fewer studies have been devoted to the specificity of breathing parameters in contributing to the physiological differentiation of several discrete, non-pathological emotions (e.g. Feleky, 1916; Ax, 1953; Stevenson and Ripley, 1952; Bloch & Santibañez, 1972; Svebak, 1975).

The present study is focused on quantifying the respiratory parameters which characterize each of six basic emotions. Recordings of the respiratory movements were done in subjects who had learned in previous workshop conditions to express these emotions by reproducing the corresponding effector patterns, i.e., the prototypical actions as defined by Santibañez & Bloch (1986). This study is part of a larger investigation concerning the properties of the Emotional Effector patterns and their relationship to genuine emotional states.

# METHODS

### Subjects

Subjects were 12 male and 24 female Danish theatre students, aged 20 to 28 years and recruited from the first and second year of the TEATERKLANEN in Copenhagen, Denmark.

### Previous workshop training

All subjects had previously learned to reproduce the "Emotional Effector patterns" described by Bloch and Santibañez (1972), during special workshop sessions under the guidance of one of us (S.B.). This special learning together with relaxation techniques, breathing exercises and general body training was part of the actor's regular theatre practice, and took place 6-8 months before the actual experimental recording sessions started. During the workshops, global indications were given with respect to respiratory rhythms, degrees of muscular tension/relaxation, degrees of eye and/or mouth opening and postural attitudes that were prototypical for each basic emotion. These indications were given in simple and colloquial terms and are roughly reproduced below:

*Anger.* "…breathe sharply in and out through the nose; keep your lips tightly closed and contract the lower jaw; focus your eyes, tensing the lids; put tension in the body and incline it slightly forwards as if ready to attack…"

*Fear.* "…give sharp in-breaths through the open mouth, 'holding' as it were, your breath; keep the breathing shallow and irregular; at the same time open your eyes wide; tense the body inclining it slightly backwards, as if trying to avoid something…"

*Sadness-crying.* "…inhale in brief saccades through the nose and then exhale all the air in one expiratory movement through the open mouth, as in a sigh; keep your body relaxed, arms hanging; let your head drop slightly and point your gaze downwards…"

*Joy-laughter.* "…inhale sharply through the nose and exhale the air through the mouth in rapid saccades; at the same time stretch your lips horizontally drawing the corners up and back; keep your eyes semi-closed, the body very relaxed, the head loosely hanging backwards…"

*Erotic love.* "…breathe in and out through the mouth, keep the body very relaxed, head tilted backwards and to the side, exposing the neck; move your hips very slowly…"

*Tenderness.* "…breathe very evenly through the nose; put up a little smile; keep your eyes open with relaxed lids. Slightly tilt your head sideways. Keep your body very relaxed…"

The actors practiced with these prototypical actions for short periods interspaced with other theatrical work. The emotional reproduction always started with the breathing prototype, as can be seen by the instructions given to the subjects. Each pattern was repeated many times in different days, but never at one time for periods longer than 2 min. The reproduction always ended with a special 'step-out' procedure (see below). The patterns were practiced in sitting or standing positions, alone or in interaction with the other actors. Well-trained actors could initiate and end the reproduction of any of the six patterns in a rapid and controlled way. A more detailed description of the entire training method is published elsewhere (Bloch et al., 1987).

## *Experimental protocol*

Once in the laboratory, subjects were informed that during the experimental session they would be asked to reproduce, with the maximum intensity possible, the prototypical emotional patterns they had learned in the workshops and to maintain them until the 'step-out' signal was given. No further instructions about how to do these patterns were given. All subjects agreed to have their physiological reactions recorded and their expressions filmed during the emotional reproduction.

Recordings were made with the subject sitting on a straight chair placed in a sound-deadened temperature-controlled and normally lighted room. The belt and electrodes were attached and, after assessing that the recording conditions were satisfactory, the experimenter gave the following standard instruction: «I would like you to breathe very evenly and to try to have a neutral expression, as neutral as possible and to stay very relaxed.» After about 10 min in these baseline 'neutral' conditions, the subject was told as follows «Keep your neutral state until I give you the signal to start reproducing one of the emotional patterns». A few seconds later the verbal signal with the name of the emotional pattern was given followed by the interjection «now» (for example «Anger, now!). The subject immediately initiated the reproduction of the corresponding respiratory-facial-postural prototypical actions for a period varying between 1 and 1.5 min, until the verbal signal of 'step-out' was given. At this signal the subject had to stop the emotional reproduction instantaneously and give two or three deep abdomino-thoracic breathing cycles and then to change posture (stretching arms and legs and touching the face). The subject was then told to reassume a regular calm breathing rhythm and to adopt again a neutral expression. A complete session included the reproduction of the six emotional patterns: anger, fear-anxiety, joy-laughter, sadness-crying, erotic love and tenderness in a randomly assigned order, plus periods of neutral «non-emotional» control states.

## *Apparatus and recordings*

Respiratory movements were recorded on a Beckman type R 411 Dynograph recorder at a paper speed of 5 mm/s, by means of a Palmer type UFI strain gauge transducer ($\pm$ 1000 g range) attached to a slightly elastic belt placed around the waist and connected to a type 9803 coupler (bandwidth DC to 120 Hz at pen level). At the beginning of each recording session the tightness of the belt and the gain of the amplifier were adjusted so that a demanded maximal inspiratory/expiratory cycle would produce a pen deflection of 50 mm. No further belt adjustments were made throughout the experimental session. Moderate changes in posture did not modify the extent of the pen deflections.

In order to check the general degree of muscular tension (without aiming at any quantitative evaluation), direct activity of the trapezius muscle was recorded from a pair of silver/silver-chloride Beckman skin electrodes (inter-electrode resistance smaller than 10 Kohms). This muscle was chosen because it is not directly involved in respiratory movements but is particularly sensitive to global changes in muscular tonus (B. Kapitaniak, personal communication).

Finally to follow up the expressive features of the emotional reproduction, subjects were videotaped on a Sony system (SL-F1F; HVC-300S) simultaneously with the polygraphic recordings. The event marker of the polygraph was coupled with a small light placed on the subject's head in order to synchronize polygraphic and video recordings. Analysis of these expressive elements is not presented here.

## *Data sampling*

From the 36 subjects who participated in these experiments, eight had to be eliminated because they were unable to produce even and regular respiratory movements for the neutral control determinations or because of technical difficulties during recordings.

For the quantitative evaluation of the respiratory parameters, only those that reproduced emotional patterns which contained the learned prototypical respiratory-facial-postural elements were considered. For this purpose, three independent judges viewed all the video sequences and rated them on a 1-10 scale according to the presence of the prototypical expressive elements. A good agreement was found between judges as shown by the significant linear correlations between the three ratings ($P < 0.001$). The same judges then checked whether the corresponding electromyographic tracings were in accordance with the basically 'tense' character of anger and fear as opposed to the 'relaxed' character of tenderness, erotic love, joy and sadness. Finally, the respiratory tracings corresponding to the selected video sequences were evaluated by the judges who visually compared the tracings with the corresponding schematized prototypical breathing configurations (see Fig. 1, c) rating them on a 1 to 10 scale. Good agreement was again found between the three judges (linear correlations $P < 0.01$). Those respiratory tracings which obtained ratings between 7 and 10 were retained for quantification. Because there were only 11 well evaluated respiratory patterns for fear (the most difficult breathing to be reproduced), 11 sequences were randomly selected for each emotion.

## Measurements and data scoring

Respiratory tracings were hand scored for the quantification of the different parameters. Two kinds of respiratory movements were considered: the fundamental cycles defined as those respiratory cycles in which the pen returned to the maximal expiratory level and the saccadic movements which were superposed on the fundamental cycles and consequently did not attain the maximal expiratory level.

For the fundamental cycles, amplitudes (A), were measured between the peak of an inspiration and the level of the pen at the end of the expiratory phase of the preceding breath, expressed in mm (Fig. 2.1). The level of reference of the obtained values was the 50 mm pen deflection determined at the beginning of each session for a maximum inspiratory/expiratory cycle. Respiratory rate was expressed as the number of fundamental cycles per minute. The duration of the inspiratory phase ($T_i$) was taken from the onset to the peak of an inspiration, except in the case of fear where $T_i$ includes the periods of maintained inspiratory levels (Fig. 2.3). Duration of the expiratory phase ($T_e$) was taken from the end of the inspiratory phase until the onset of the next breath. In 82% of neutral control recordings, the expiratory phase included a period in which no expiratory movements could be detected. This parameter, which will be referred to as 'expiratory pause' (P), was scored as a percentage of $T_e$ (Fig. 2.1).

For the saccadic respiratory movements only amplitude and rate were quantified. Amplitudes (a) were obtained by measuring peak to peak pen deflections expressed in mm (Figs. 2.2 and 2.3) and rates by counting the number of saccadic peaks and expressing it in cycles/min.

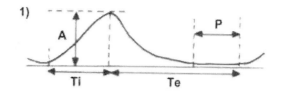
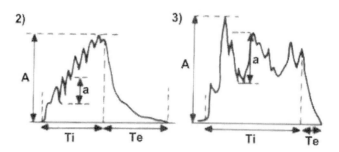

Fig. 2. Schematic illustration of how respiratory parameters were measured. Three cases are shown: (1) a simple fundamental cycle, (2) a fundamental cycle with saccasic movements superposed on the inspiratory phase (typical of the breathing pattern of sadness-crying) and (3) a fundamental cycle with a maintained inspiratory level and superposed irregular saccadic movements (typical of the breathing patterns of fear). Abbreviations: A, amplitude of the fundamental cycle, a, amplitude of the superposed saccadic movements; $T_o$ inspiratory time, $T_e$ expiratory time; P, 'expiratory pause', corresponding to a period where no repiratory movements could be observed.

# RESULTS

## *Dynamics of the emotional reproduction*

Subjects had been asked at the start of the experimental session to reproduce the respiratory-facial-postural prototypical actions in their most intense form. It was, however, observed that as the reproduction went along, recordings both of the respiratory movements as well as of the expressive elements showed a temporal evolution. This is illustrated for respiration in Fig. 3, which ex-amplifies typical recordings of respiratory changes after the «Now» signal had been given. We have distinguished for each respiratory recording an initial phase (dotted underlinings) in which the prototypical respiratory patterns were reproduced as learned, in a 'robot-like' fashion; a second phase in which respiratory movements became less stereotyped while losing neither their basic structure nor their intensity, and a third phase during which the respiratory patterns became more irregular and were generally modified by spontaneous vocalizations. As the respiratory patterns evolved, the expressive features also became clearer and better defined.

This evolution of the emotional reproduction was assessed in a separate recognition study done in our laboratory (Aguilera et al., 1989). The test consisted in presenting 10-s mute video clips of the reproduced emotional patterns to 24 non-adverted observers who had to identify which of the six emotions was being portrayed and to scale their degree of certitude. Results showed that if video clips taken during the first 10 s of reproduction (first phase) were presented, recognition scores were 64%. When clips corresponding to 10 s taken at the end of the second phase were presented, recognition scores were significantly higher (88%, $P < 0.05$) and had a greater degree of certitude ($P < 0.01$).

## *Quantitative analysis of the respiratory parameters*

*Changes in respiratory movements during emotional reproduction.* Quantification was done during the second phase of emotional reproduction over periods of about 20 s (Fig. 3, black underlinings) immediately preceding the beginning of the third phase. In this way neither the initial purely 'robot-like' phase nor the episode corresponding to vocalizations were included in the quantitative analysis. Depending on the respiratory rate the analyzed sequences covered between 3 to 14 fundamental cycles.

Respiratory movements were also quantified for each subject over 3-5 cycles corresponding to 'neutral' non-emotional states preceding each emotional reproduction. These recordings covered periods during which subjects maintained a regular, rhythmic breathing rate (13.6 cy/min average), low levels of muscular activity and 'neutral' facial and postural expressions. Average values of these measurements gave the neutral control value for each individual.

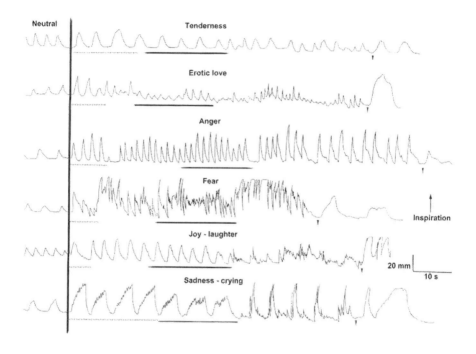

*Fig. 3. Typical recordings of the respiratory movements showing the dynamics of each emotional reproduction preceded by periods of neutral 'non-emotional' breathing. The vertical line indicates the beginning of the emotional reproduction. The evolution of the breathing pattern has been divided into three phases. The first corresponds to the initial learned prototypical patterns (dotted underlinings). Quantitative measurements were done during 20 s periods (black underlinings) at the end of the second phase in which respiratory movements appear less stereotyped. The period immediately following (third phase) is usually accompanied by spontaneous vocalizations. Downward arrow tips indicate the 'step-out' signal, the emotional reproduction ending abruptly (see text). The duration of each phase varies according to the subject and the type of emotion.*

*Bottom right corner: scales for pen deflection (in mm) and time (in s).*

## TABLE 1

*Mean values ( ± S.E.M.) of respiratory parameters (fundamental breathing cycles) for each emotional reproduction as compared (Student's paired t-test) to the corresponding neutral control values (in brackets)*

| Emotion | Respiratory parameters of the fundamental cycles | | | |
|---|---|---|---|---|
| | amplitude (mm) | rate (Cy / min) | pause (%Tn) | Ti/Te |
| Tenderness | 12.8±1.8 | 12.9±1.6 | 20.5±3.5 | 0.57±0.07 |
| | (14.2±1.5) | (13.8±1.5) | (14.6±3.8) | (0.56±0.07) |
| Erotic Love* | 17.8±1.9 | 15.2±1.9 | 5.2±1.8 * | 0.73±0.01 |
| | (13.9±1.4) | (12.8±1.2) | (18.7±3.9) | (0.60±0.04) |
| Anger | 33.6±3.1 | 33.1±3.9 *** | 0 *** | 0.69±0.10 |
| | (12.0±0.9) | (12.8±1.2) | (17.9±5.1) | (0.54±0.05) |
| Joy-laugh | 29.4±2.0 *** | 9.6±0.9 * | 7.7±2.4 | 0.38±0.05 *** |
| | (12.2±1.1) | (13.4±1.4) | (14.5±3.4) | (0.63±0.03) |
| Sadness-cry | 27.7±3.0 *** | 11.4±0.9 * | 7.8±2.8 | 0.99±0.14 * |
| | (10.8±1.5) | (14.7±1.2) | (16.2±3.7) | (0.63±0.14) |
| Fear | 38.6±2.3 *** | 7.2±1.0 ** | 0 *** | 5.60±0.90 *** |
| | (10.2±1.0) | (14.1±1.2) | (18.9±3.9) | (0.55±0.40) |

\* P < 0.05, \*\* P < 0.01, \*\*\* P< 0.001

Table 1 presents mean values of respiratory amplitudes and rates, duration of expiratory pause and inspiratory time/expiratory time ratios (Ti/Te), of the fundamental cycles during each emotional reproduction. The corresponding control values are shown within brackets. During tenderness no significant changes were observed with respect to neutral though the expiratory pause was slightly longer. During erotic love the expiratory pause was significantly shortened (paired «t» test, t(10) = 3.10, P < 0.02) or absent, and slight but not significant increases in amplitude and rate were observed. By contrast, breathing during anger was quite different from neutral, with highly significant increases in amplitude (t(10) = 5.10, P < 0.001) and rate (t(10) = 5.61, P < 0.01) and a total absence of expiratory pause. No changes in Ti/Te were observed for any of these three emotional breathing patterns. During joy-laughter and sadness-crying, amplitude was significantly increased (t(10) > 6.22, P < 0.001 for both patterns) while rate decreased (t(10) = 2.25 and 2.26, respectively, P < 0.05). During fear the increase in amplitude and the decrease in respiratory rate (for the fundamental cycle) were both highly significant ($t(10) = 11.17$, $p < 0.001$ and $t(10) = 4.45$, $P < 0.01$, respectively), the expiratory pause being systematically absent. The reduction of rate of the fundamental cycles is due to the prolonged displacement of the respiratory level towards inspiration, largely increasing Ti, which is characteristic of the breathing pattern of fear. For these last three emotional patterns different changes appear for Ti/Te ratios: a significant decrease for joy-laughter ($t(10) = 3.86$, $P < 0.001$), a slight increase for sadness-crying ($t(10) = 2.50$, $P < 0.05$) and a large increase for fear ($t(10) = 5.59$, $P < 0.001$).

The emotions of joy-laughter, sadness-crying and fear were further characterized by the presence of respiratory saccadic movements superposed on the fundamental cycles. In the case of sadness-crying saccadic movements of low amplitude ($6.90 \pm 1.0$) and high rate ($180.0 \pm 26.8$) were superposed on the inspiratory phase. In the case of joy-laughter saccadic movements of low amplitude ($4.15 \pm 0.6$ mm) and high rate ($154.2 \pm 15.3$ c/min) were superposed on the expiratory phase. With respect to fear, irregular saccadic movements of larger amplitude ($17.5 \pm 2.7$ mm) and lower rate ($75.9 \pm 8.1$ c/min) than those of joy and sadness were superposed mainly on the periods of maintained inspiratory level. Moreover, "tremor-like" movements of small amplitudes ($4.40 \pm 0.7$ mm) and very high rates ($253.6 \pm 35.7$ c/min) were frequently recorded for this emotional reproduction.

## *Comparisons between the six emotional breathing patterns*

Fig. 4 shows, for each emotion, the set of changes in respiratory parameters of the fundamental breathing cycles. Relative changes of each parameter with respect to neutral values «emotional)-(neutral)/(neutral» were calculated for each subject. In this way, an increase from neutral values appears as a positive score, a decrease as a negative one and no change corresponds to zero or the neutral control level.

Four independent one-way within ANOVAs show that the breathing parameters are different for the six emotional patterns: for amplitude ($F(5, 60) = 11.57$, $P < 0.001$), for rate ($F(5, 60) = 17.63$, $P < 0.001$), for expiratory pause ($F(5, 60) = 4.25$, $P < 0.01$) and for Ti/Te ($F(5, 60) = 42.76$, $P < 0.001$). Planned paired comparisons between emotions (Newman-Keuls procedure) give the respective levels of significance (Table II).

APPENDIX I 197

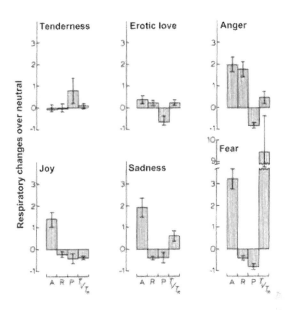

Fig. 4. Histograms showing, for the fundamental cycles, means (+S.E.M.) of individual relative changes ((emotional)-(neutral/neutral)) for each repiratory parameter (see text). Abbreviations: A, amplitude; R, rate; P, duration of the expiratory pause and Ti/Te, ratios of inspiratory over expiratory time.

### Amplitude

|   | T | E | A | J | S | F |
|---|---|---|---|---|---|---|
| T |   | O | ** | O | ** | ** |
| E |   |   | ** | O | O | ** |
| A |   |   |   | O | O | ** |
| J |   |   |   |   | O | ** |
| S |   |   |   |   |   | ** |
| F |   |   |   |   |   |   |

### Rate

|   | T | E | A | J | S | F |
|---|---|---|---|---|---|---|
| T |   | O | * | O | O | O |
| E |   |   | * | O | O | O |
| A |   |   |   | ** | ** | ** |
| J |   |   |   |   | O | O |
| S |   |   |   |   |   | O |
| F |   |   |   |   |   |   |

### Pause

|   | T | E | A | J | S | F |
|---|---|---|---|---|---|---|
| T |   | ** | ** | ** | ** | ** |
| E |   |   | O | O | O | O |
| A |   |   |   | O | O | O |
| J |   |   |   |   | O | O |
| S |   |   |   |   |   | O |
| F |   |   |   |   |   |   |

### Ti/Te

|   | T | E | A | J | S | F |
|---|---|---|---|---|---|---|
| T |   | O | O | O | O | ** |
| E |   |   | O | O | O | ** |
| A |   |   |   | O | O | ** |
| J |   |   |   |   | O | ** |
| S |   |   |   |   |   | ** |
| F |   |   |   |   |   |   |

O n.s., *p<0.05, **p<0.01

Table II
Planned paired comparisons between emotions (Newman-Keuls procedure) corresponding to data presented inn Fig. 5., for each repiratory parameter.

As can be seen from Fig. 4 and Table II, the sets of changes in the respiratory parameters strongly differed from one emotional reproduction to the other:

*Tenderness* was the only emotional pattern during which the expiratory pause increased, this change being significantly different from the decreases observed for all other emotions. The small changes in amplitude, rate and Ti/Te with respect to neutral values constitute the other main features of this breathing pattern.

*Erotic love* breathing, though resembling that of tenderness in its general configuration, was significantly differentiated by a larger amplitude (separate ANOVA, $F(1, 20) = 4.37, P < 0.05$) and by the absence of expiratory pause. Moreover moderate changes in amplitude, rate and *Ti/Te* globally distinguished erotic breathing from that of anger, sadness, joy and fear.

*Anger* breathing was characterized by strong increases in both respiratory rate and amplitude. The increase in rate was significantly different from the changes in rate of all other emotions. The increase in amplitude was quantitatively similar to those of joy and sadness and significantly different from those of erotic love and fear. The expiratory pause was absent.

*Joy-laughter* breathing was characterized by an increase in the duration of the inspiratory phase which resulted in a decrease in *Ti/Te*. This change significantly differentiated this emotion from sadness, erotic love and anger (separate ANOVAs $F(1, 20) = 14.82, P < 0.001$; $F(1, 20) = 19.57, P < 0.001; F(1, 20) = 8.11, P < 0.01$, respectively).

*Sadness-crying* was characterized by an increase in the duration of the inspiratory phase which resulted in an increase in *Ti/Te*. Otherwise it was quantitatively very similar to that of joy with respect to amplitude, rate and expiratory pause.

*Fear* breathing differed significantly from that of all other emotions by a very large increase in both amplitude and *Ti/Te*. This last parameter varied over a large range since the sustained inspiratory level could have different durations as a result of the typical irregularity of this breathing. Moreover, the expiratory pause was totally absent.

It should be remembered that the presence of saccadic superposed movements in these last three emotional breathing patterns, were further elements of differentiation among the six emotions.

## DISCUSSION

In the present study we have quantitatively characterized the breathing configurations of six basic emotions: joy-laughter, sadness-crying, fear-anxiety, anger, erotic love and tenderness. The reported data were obtained from subjects who had previously learned to express these emotions by reproducing the corresponding prototypical respiratory-facial-postural actions as extracted from genuine emotional states (Bloch & Santibañez, 1972; Santibañez & Bloch, 1986). Results show significant changes in respiratory parameters for each emotional reproduction. For emotions with rather simple breathing configurations, characterized by a rhythmic repetition of the fundamental cycles (tenderness, erotic love and anger), the main respiratory parameters of differentiation are changes in amplitudes respiratory rate and duration of the expiratory pause, some of these parameters with a high level of significance. For emotions whose main breathing configurations are characterized by the presence of saccadic respiratory movements superposed to the fundamental cycles (joy-laughter, sadness-crying and fear-anxiety), $Ti/Te$ ratios are the major parameters of differentiation.

It could be argued that the quantitative respiratory differences reported were due to differences in the intensity of each emotional reproduction. This is highly improbable since the prototypical actions of these effector patterns had been extracted from intensely relived emotional episodes (Bloch & Santibañez, 1972), and subjects had been expressly requested during the experimental recordings to reproduce them in their strongest possible form.

It is necessary to confront the reported breathing configurations and respiratory parameters with those obtained by other investigators. Such comparisons are often difficult to establish due to the different methodologies used to produce an emotional state, the various procedures for recording respiration and the different criteria for measuring the respiratory changes. In view of this diversity of approaches only rough and descriptive comparisons can be made.

Most investigations about the relationship between breathing and emotion have been concerned with stress and anxiety. In clinical descriptions anxiety is usually associated with breathlessness, «suspirious respiration», «inability to get enough air into the lungs» (Christie, 1935; Stevenson & Ripley, 1952; Bass & Gardner, 1985a). In fact the difficulty in breathing reported by anxious patients as a common accompaniment of anxiety represents what Freud (1894/1962) termed an anxiety 'equivalent'. Frequent breath-holds and sighs have also been reported during genuine distress (Heim et al., 1968). On the other hand hyperventilation or overbreathing has been frequently associated with phobic and panic disorders (Garssen et al., 1983; King, 1988; Bass & Gardner, 1985 b); Freeman et al., 1986), the sudden experience of hyperventilation actually preceding the subjective experience of fear (Ley, 1985).

Other aspects of respiratory function during fear-anxiety have been analyzed experimentally. For instance anticipation of an electric shock during a perceptual task induces a decrease in end-tidal $CO_2$ and an increase in respiratory rate, conversely $CO_2$ levels increase during quiet states (Suess et al., 1980); manipulation of threat during task performance induces a temporal shift of the peak effect of the respiratory change (Sveback, 1986); abdomino-diaphragmatic breathing is enhanced during relaxation and suppressed under conditions of emotional strain (Faulkner, 1941); mental tasks or negative effects are accompanied predominantly by thoracic breathing, while breathing movements during relaxation and positive affect are predominantly abdominal (Ancoli & Kamiya, 1979; Sveback et al., 1981). Changes in respiratory parameters that are more directly related to our own data have also been reported, such as significant increases in respiratory rate just before parachute jumping (Fenz & Jones, 1972); increases in rate, amplitude and *I/R* ratios (inspiratory/respiratory times) during experimentally provoked anger or fear (Ax, 1953) and increase and a certain variability in *I/E* ratios during fear imagery (Lang et al., 1980).

The ensemble of clinical observations and experimental results are generally consistent in showing that fear-anxiety provokes irregularity of breathing, frequent periods of breath-holds, increase in minute ventilatory volume, alteration of tidal volume, increases in respiratory amplitude and rate and increases in *Ti/Te* ratio as compared to baseline conditions. The characteristic breathing configuration of the fear pattern we report is very similar to the descriptions of respiratory changes during genuine fear-anxiety. In our experimental conditions the irregular saccadic movements superposed on prolonged periods of maintained inspiratory level, account for the typical high respiratory rate and increase in *Ti/Te* ratios found during fear by the above mentioned authors.

Other emotions have been much less studied than fear. However the large increase in amplitude and rate we found during anger reproduction is in accordance with the increased amplitude and rate and elevated ventilation described by others (Feleky, 1916; Ax, 1953; Dudley et al., 1964; Stevenson and Ripley, 1952). With respect to the pattern of joy-laughter, Svebak (1975) showed that the breathing of laughter is characterized by a forceful inspiration followed by 'oscillatory' movements during expiration. These oscillations denoted by the author as 'ha-ha' responses, are only present during 'mirthful' laughter. The respiratory configuration of the effector pattern of joy-laughter we report is very similar to the one found by Sveback, our saccadic expiratory movements corresponding to his 'ha-ha' responses. Though these saccadic expirations were not described by Feleky (1916) they can be recognized by inspecting her pneumographic tracings during mimicked laughter (op. cit. pp. 235, Fig. 8). Changes in respiratory parameters associated with depression (close to our pattern of sadness) have also been reported, either appearing spontaneously during interviews (Stevenson & Ripley, 1952) or during hypnotical suggestion (Dudley et al., 1964). Finally, to our knowledge, no experimental studies of respiratory changes accompanying the emotional state of love have been reported, neither in the sexual expression of love (what we call erotic love), nor in its friendly/maternal/paternal aspects (what we call tenderness). Clynes (1975) has shown that these two forms of love have different «dynamic expressive essentic forms» and different respiratory patterns.

The work with which our respiratory data can best be confronted with is the pioneering study of Feleky (1916) who compared the respiratory changes during different emotions produced by imagery or by mimicry, concluding that emotions are principally reflected in the muscles of the face and those of respiration. She found different though not significant increases in amplitude of respiratory movements (anger > fear > pain > laughter) and different changes in $Ti/Te$ ratios (increases for fear > anger > pain and decrease for laughter). The trend of these respiratory changes is similar to our own findings.

In conclusion the breathing configuration of the Emotional Effector patterns qualitatively described by Santibañez and Bloch (1986) and quantified in the present study is in general agreement with the clinical and/or experimental studies reported by other investigators, at least for the basic emotions classically agreed upon: anger, fear-anxiety, joy-laughter and sadness-crying. These similarities are a further support for validating the selected prototypical breathing configurations as being characteristic of each emotion.

Another important observation emerges from the present study, and that concerns the dynamics of the emotional reproduction. During the recordings we observed that the breathing evolved from the learned 'robot-like' initial phase towards a less stereotyped reproduction of the respiratory movements, frequently followed by spontaneous vocalizations similar to those observed during genuine emotions. At the same time the facial expressions became better defined and more natural, as was separately assessed in a recognition study (see results section). This supports the notion that a partial activation of the emotional control system had occurred.

The hypothesis that the reproduction of an emotional effector pattern, i.e., the combined respiratory-facial-postural actions, can activate different levels of the corresponding emotional network is supported by the existence of multiple physiological interactions between the respiratory, postural and facial systems (Dejours, 1964). It has been shown, for instance, that in man reflexes originating in exercising muscles can elicit cardiovascular and respiratory responses (Alam & Smirk, 1938; Asmussen et al., 1943; Wiley & Lind, 1971; Grossman et al., 1983). An interaction of this sort also exists between facial muscle activity and lung airway resistance (Strohl et al., 1982; Glaus & Kotses, 1983) and between upper body posture and ventilation (Haas et al., 1982). Other interactions have been reported by Ekman et al. (1983), who showed that mimicking emotion specific patterns of facial actions resulted in autonomic activation partially differentiating between some basic emotions. Preliminary results from our own laboratory indicate a differential autonomic pattern of activation for the six reproduces emotional patterns (Lemeignan et al., in preparation). Moreover interactions between facial expressions and subjective experience have led to the facial feedback hypothesis which predicts a causal role for the face in the experience of emotion (see reviews by Buck, 1980 and by Adelman & Zajonc, 1989).

The increasing number of studies indicating that voluntary alterations in respiratory parameters can alter the mood of subjects in stressful situations further supports our hypothesis. For instance, patients with psychophysiological disorders displaying rapid respiratory rates and low $CO_2$ levels can improve their somatic and physiological symptoms with respiratory therapy (e.g., Clark, 1985; Grossman et al., 1985). In normal subjects, experimental manipulations of respiratory parameters indicate that pacing the respiratory rate can reduce the subjective influence of anxiogenic conditions (McCaul et al., 1979; Lande, 1982). Respiratory self-regulation however is often hindered by the difficulty some persons have in modulating respiratory muscles (Christiansen & Sveback, 1989) or in maintaining the learned respiratory modifications (Gallego & Camus, 1989).

The experimental model we propose for generating emotions based on a 'bottom-up' activation of the emotional control system, fits well into a systems theory as proposed by Schwartz (1986). This theory conceptually implies that « the subjective experience of an emotion should be more complete and more stable as more physiological elements are activated and organized in meaningful patterns» (Schwartz, 1986, pp. 374).

In the experimental conditions of the present report, the intention was not to reach the full process of emotional activation since the presence of verbalizations, vocalizations, gestures or ample body movements render quantitative determinations very difficult. In fact the emotional reproduction was systematically interrupted by a 'stepout' instruction which assured the return to a neutral control state. However the emotional activation attained was sufficient to produce well differentiated changes in respiratory parameters which are quite close to those present during intense genuine emotions. We are nevertheless aware that these quantitative results must be confronted with data obtained in 'real-life' situations. Gathering such kind of direct evidence, however, is no small challenge.

# ACKNOWLEDGEMENTS

This research was supported by the French Centre National de la Recherche Scientifique (CNRS, UA 1199). The authors gratefully acknowledge the Danish theatre students from the TEATERKLANEN, for their willingness to participate as experimental subjects in a psychophysiological study, Mario Liotti for his valuable contribution in the data analysis and interpretation and Don Tucker for his critical revision of previous versions of the manuscript.

# REFERENCES

Adelmann, P. and Zajonc, R.B. (1989) Facial efference and the experience of emotion. Annu. Rev. Psychol, 40: 249-280.

Aguilera-T., N., Lemeignan, M. and Bloch, S. (1989). Influence du sexe et du type d'émotion dans la transnmission non verbale des messages émotionnels. Proceedings of the 3ème Colloque National des Neurosciences, Montpellier, France, pp. 187.

Alam, M. and Smirk, F.H. (1938) Observations in man upon a pulse-accelerating reflex from the voluntary muscles of the legs. J. Physiol, (London) 92: 167-177.

Alexander, F. and Saul, L.J. (1940) Respiration and personality–a preliminary report: part I. Description of the curves. Psychosom. Med., 11: 110-118.

Ancoli, S. and Kamiya, J. (1979) Respiratory patterns during emotional expression. Biofeedback and Self-regulation, 2242.

Asmussen, E., Nielsen, M. and Wieth-Pedersen, G. (1943) Cortical or reflex control of respiration during muscular work? Acta PhysioL Scand., 6: 168-175.

Ax, A.F. (1953) The physiological differentiation between fear and anger in humans. Psychosom. Med., 15: 433-442.

Bass, C. and Gardner, W. (1985 a) Emotional influences on breathing and breathlessness. J. Psychosom. Res., 29: 599-609.

Bass, C. and Gardner, W. (1985 b) Respiratory and psychiatric abnormalities in chronic symptomatic hyperventilation. Br. Med. J., 1: 1387-1390.

Bloch, S. (1989) Effector patterns of basic human emotions: an experimental model for emotional induction. Behav. Brain Res., 33: 330.

Bloch, S., Orthous, P. and Santibañez-H, G. (1987) Effector patterns of basic emotion: a Psychophysiological Method for Training Actors. J. Soc. Biol. Struct., 10: 1-19.

Bloch, S. and Santibabez-H, G. (1972) Training of emotional «effection» in humans: significance of its feedback on subjectivity. In: S. Bloch and R. Aneiros (Eds.), Simposio Latinoamericano de Psicobiologia del Aprendizaje, Santiago, Chile: Publ. Fac. Med., Universidad de Chile, pp. 170-184.

Buck, R. (1980) Nonverbal behavior and the theory of emotion: the facial feedback hypothesis. J. Pers. Soc. Psychol, 38: 811-824.

Buck, R., Miller, R.E. and Caul, W.F. (1974) Sex, personality, and physiological variables in communication of emotion via facial expression. J. Pers. Soc. Psychol, 30: 587-596.

Christiansen, B. (1965) Studies in respiration and personality. Institute of Social Rescarch, Oslo.

Christiansen, B. and Svebak, S. (1989) The role of psychopathology and gender in respiratory self-regulation. Scand. J. Psychol, 30: 146-154.

Christie, R.V. (1935) Some types of respiration in the neuroses. Q.J. Med., 16: 427-434.

Clark, D.M., Salkovskis, P.M. and Chalkley, A.J. (1985) Respiratory control as a treatment of panic attack. Percept. Motor Skills, 16: 23-30.

Clynes, M. (1975) Communication and generation of emotion through essentic form. In: Emotions-Their Parameters and Measurement, L. Levi (Ed.), Raven Press, New York pp. 588-589.

Damas-Mora, J., Grant, L., Kenyon, P., Patel, M.K. and Jenner, F.A. (1976) Respiratory ventilation and carbon dioxide levels in syndromes of depression. Br. J. Psychiatry, 129: 457-469.

Damas-Mora, J., Souster, L. and Jenner, F.A. (1982) Diminished hypercapnic drive in endogenous or severs depression. J. Psychosom. Res., 26: 237-245.

Dejours, P. (1964) Control of respiration in muscular exercise. In W.o. Fenn and H. Rahn (Eds.) Handbook of physiology, Section 3, Respiration, Vol. I, Washington DC, American Physiological Society.

Duclos, S.E., Laird, J.D., Schneider, E., Sexter, M., Stern, L, and Van Lighten, 0. (1989) Emotion-specific effects of facial expressions and postures on emotional experience. J. Personality Soc. Psychol., 57: 100-108.

Dudley, D.L. and Pitts-Poarch (1980) Psychophysiological aspects of respiratory control. Clin. Chest Med., 1: 131-143.

Dudley, D.L., Holmes, T.H., Martin, C.J. and Ripley, H.S. (1964) Changes in respiration associated with hypnotically induced emotion, pain and exercise. Psychosom. Med., 26: 46-57.

Ekman, P. and Friesen, W. (1967) Head and body cues in the judgment of emotions: a reformulation. Percept. Mot. Skills, 24: 711-724.

Ekman, P., Levenson, R.W. and Friesen, W.V. (1983) Autonomic nervous system activity distinguishes among emotions. Science, 221: 1208-1210.

Ekman, P. and Oster, H. (1979) Facial expressions of emotion. Annu. Rev. Psychol., 30: 527-554.

Faulkner, W.B. (1941) Effects of the emotions upon diaphragmatic function. Psychosom. Med., 3: 187-189.

Feleky, A. (1916) The influence of the emotions on respiration. J. Exp. Psychol., 1: 218-241.

Fenz, W.D. and Jones, G.B. (1972) Individual differences in physiologic arousal and performance in sport parachutists. Psychosom. Med., 34: 1-8.

Finesinger, J.E. (1944) The effect of pleasant and unpleasant ideas on the respiratory pattern (spirogram) in psychoneurotic patients. Am. J. Psychiatry, 100: 659-667.

Freeman, L.J., Conway, A.V. and Nixon, P.G.F. (1986) Heart rate response, emotional disturbance and hyperventilation. J. Psychosom. Res., 30: 429-436.

Freud, S. (1962) On the grounds for detaching a particular syndrome from neurasthenia under the description «anxiety neurosis». In The Standard Edition of the Complete Psychological Works of Sigmund Freud.

Vol. IIL Early Psycho-analytic Publications. London: The Hogart Press (Originally published 1894).

Fridlund, A., Schwartz, G. and Fowler, S. (1984) Pattern recognition of self-reported emotional state from multiplesite facial EMG activity during affective imagery. Psychophysiology, 21: 622-636.

Gallego, J. and Camus, J.F. (1989) Optimization of informative feedback in ventilatory pattern learning. Eur. Bull Cogn. Psychol., 9: 505-520.

Garssen, B., Van Weenendaal, W. and Bloemink, R. (1983) Agoraphobia and the hyperventilation syndrome. Behav. Res. Therap., 21: 643-649.

Glaus, K.D. and Kotses, H. (1983) Facial muscle tension influences lung airway resistance; lirnb muscle tension does not. Biol. Psychol., 17: 105-120.

Grossman, P. (1983) Respiration, stress, and cardiovascular function. Psychophysiology, 20: 284-300.

Grossman, P., De Swart, J.C.G. and Defares, P.B. (1985) A controlled study of a breathing therapy of hyperventilation syndrome. J. Psychosom. Res., 29: 49-58.

Haas, F., Simnowitz, M., Axen, K., Gaudino, D. and Hass, A. (1982) Effect of upper body posture on forced inspiration and expiration. J. Appl. Physiol., 52: 879-886.

Heim, E., Knapp, P.H., Vachon, L., Globus, G.G. and Nemetz, S.i. (1968) Emotion, breathing and speech. Psychosom. Med., 12: 261-274.

Izard, C. (1971) The face of emotion. NY. Appleton-Century Crofts.

King, J.C. (1988) Hyperventilation- a therapist's point of view: discussion paper. J. Roy. Soc. Med., 81: 532-536.

Kudoh, T. and Matsumoto, D. (1985) Cross-cultural examination of the semantic dimensions of body postures. J. Pers. and Soc. Psychol, 55: 36-42.

Lande, S.D. (1982) Physiological and subjective measures of anxiety during flooding. Behav. Res. Therap., 20: 81-88.

Lang, P.J., Kozak, M.J., Miller, G.A., Levin, D.N. and McLean, A. (Jr) (1980) Emotional imagery: conceptual structure and pattern of somato-visceral response. Psychophysiology, 17: 179-192.

Ley, R. (1985) Agoraphobia, the panic attack and the hyperventilation syndrome. Behav. Res. Therap., 23: 79-81,

McCaul, K., Solomon, S. and Holmes, D. (1979) Effects of paced respiration on physiological responses to threat. J. Pers. Soc. Psychol. 37: 564-571.

Mehrabian, A. (1968) Inference of attitude from the posture, orientation and distance of a communicator. J. Consult. Clin. Psychol., 32: 296-308.

Rinn, W.E. (1984) The neuropsychology of facial expression: a review of the neurological and psychological mechanisms for producing facial expressions. Psychol. Bull., 95: 52-77.

Riskind, J.H. (1984) They stoop to conquer: guiding and self-regulatory functions of physical posture after success and failure. J. Pers. Soc. Psychol, 47: 479-493.

Rosser, R. and Guz, A. (1981) Psychological approaches to breathlessness and its treatment. J. Psychosom. Res., 25:439-447.

Santibañez-H.G. and Bloch, S. (1986) A qualitative analysis of Emotional Effector patterns and their feedback. Pav. J. Biol. Sci., 21: 108-116.

Schwartz, G.E. (1986) Emotion and psychophysiological organization: a systems approach. In: M.G.M. Coles, E. Donchin and S.W. Porges (Eds.), The Guilford Press, New York, 354-377.

Schwartz, G.E., Weinberger, D.A. and Singer, J.A. (1981) Cardiovascular differentiation of happiness, sadness, anger and fear following imagery and exercise. Psychosom. Med., 4: 343-364.

Shea, S.A., Walter, J., Murphy, K. and Guz, A. (1987) Evidence for individuality of breathing patterns in resting healthy man. Resp. PhysioL, 68: 331-344.

Smith, C., McHugo, G. and Lanzetta, J. (1986) The facial muscle patterning of posed and imagery-induced expressions by expressive posers. Motivation and Emotion, 10: 133-157.

Sogon, S. and Masutani, M. (1989) Identification of emotion from body movements: a cross-cultural study of americans and japanese. Psychol. Rep., 65: 35-46.

Stevenson, I. and Ripley, H.S. (1952) Variations in respiration and in respiratory symptoms during changes in emotion. Psychosom. Med., 14: 476-490.

Strohl, K.P., O'Cain, C.F. and Slutsky, A.S. (1982) Alae nasi activation and nasal resistance in healthy subjects. J. Appl. Physiol.: Respirat. Environ. Exercise Physiol., 52: 1432-1437.

Suess, W.M., Alexander, A.B., Smith, D.D., Sweeney, H.W. and Marion, R.J. (1980) The effects of psychological stress on respiration: a preliminary study of anxiety and hyperventilation. Psychophysiology, 17: 535-540.

Svebak, S. (1975) Respiratory patterns as predictors of laughter. Psychophysiology, 12: 21-29.

Svebak, S. (1986) Patterns of cardiovascular-somatic-respiratory interactions in the continuous perceptual-motor task paradigm. In P. Grossman, K.H.L. Janssen and D. Vaitl (Eds.), Cardiorespiratory and cardiosomatic psychophysiology, Plenum, New York, pp. 219-230.

Svebak, S., Dalen, K. and Storfjell, o. (1981) The psychological significance of task-induced tonic changes in somatic and autonomic activity. Psychophysiology, 18: 403-409.

Wagner, H.L., Mac Donald, C.J. and Manstead, A.S.R. (1986) Communication of individual emotions by spontaneous facial expressions. J. Pers. Soc. Psychol., 50: 737-743.

Wiley, R.L. and Lind, A.R. (1971) Respiratory responses to sustained static contractions in humans. Clin. Sci., 40: 221-234.

# APPENDIX II
# THE SCRIPT OF THE ALBA EMOTING FILM*

This film was made in Andalusia in the south of Spain in March, 1990. The place chosen to film was the small town called Capileira in the Alpujarras, a mountainous area in the Costa del Sol near Granada. The architecture of the buildings in the towns in this area is pre-Phoenician with a later Arabic influence: houses made of stone, with terraced roofs on which people circulate from one house to the other, vegetable gardens, terraced gardens, almond and chestnut orchards, water everywhere.

The settings of the film are two: the fireplace inside one of these houses, and outside, a natural stage; a huge threshing floor where in old times horses walked round and round a track grinding grain into flour with their hooves.

Lost stone walls, the threshing floor stage, the cold, the fire, the Spanish tapas at mid-day; discussions trying to reconcile science and art, the speech on the threshing stage; the inserted shots of different activities and workshops of *Alba Emoting* around the world. Nights without sleeping, filming, laughing, fighting, weeping; the constant, powerful sounds of Flamenco always in the background hovering over the creative activity of these gypsy filmmakers.

---

* In the spirit of this book it is absolutely fitting for the author to include the script of the film the author made with Pedro Sándor after the scientific article she has written. This script is actually a post script, a free version written as the pen flowed that Susana did while she viewed the film. It seems to her to be highly satisfactory because it communicates her internal, subjective feelings and convictions about the subject of *Alba Emoting*.

This is the atmosphere in which the film was made and that is communicated by the film. It begins with the image of El Zorro –that's me– with the soul and the hat, a crooked mask, the eye of a cat, the transparent knife, the sensual challenge of throwing down the gauntlet. The music: the strong masculine Flamenco song alternating with feminine operatic arias.

My transcription of the sound-track follows:

Three orchestral chords:
> Pa pam
>> Pa pam
>>> Pa pam

ALBA AVICINA...
> (Dawn is coming...
>> Emoting with ALBA)

A face appears with a mask saying in French:
> *Il existe un sentiment pour chaque souffle*
(An emotion exists for each breath)

The eye is covered with a magnifying glass; while the lips say mysteriously:
> *Il faut trouver quel sentiment correspond a quel souffle*
(It is necessary to find which emotion corresponds to each breath.)

A transparent spade emerges while the voice whispers hoarsely but lightly:
> *Il faut pénetrer le sentimenet par le souffle*
(It is necessary to penetrate the emotion with the breath)

The hand goes up and puts the hat on the head while the voice in the background pierces the air with divine trills. The woman smiles, slowly removes her glove, and throws it as a challenge saying:

> *This is the story of scientific research that discovered a love-affair between Breathing and Emotion.*

Clouds appear in the sky and the chords of a virile, masculine gypsy lament are heard.

*Ay ay yay*
 *Que donde la he visto yo,*
  *Su carita llorosa*
   *Diciendo mujer hermosa*
    *La que tieneee,*
     *La que tieene el español.*

Title hanging from the clouds:

## *Alba*
## *Emoting*

The camera descends from the sky, moves over the roofs of the stone houses, and penetrates into an Andalusian patio.

In the foreground a girl weeps, breathing in interrupted breaths through her nose while she holds a fan.

A man weeps with all his heart, contracting his eyes, against a Mozart background.

Inside, you see the creeping flames in the fireplace. A voice-over whispers:

## *Emoting*

In the foreground the face of Susana is saying to the viewers:

*The crying of Camila and Julian that you just saw was not acting, or the result of sad images or the memories of personal sad situations. What they were doing was to reproduce the special breathing which we found is connected with the emotion of sadness and which I taught them to do: Saccadic in-breathing through the nose followed by one out-breath through the open mouth, as in a sigh* (She shows how it is done).

*This is sadness, or crying.*

Foreground shot of Susana with her head inclined saying:

*To make them cry in this way, is an original procedure for emotional induction.*

Again a mysterious voice-over whispers over the flames:

## 𝔈𝔪𝔬𝔱𝔦𝔫𝔤 ...

Foreground shot, SB saying very seriously, with the background of musical chords

*We discovered, for the purpose of science, in Santiago de Chile, a special way of breathing, specific for each basic emotion.*

Change of shot, now, SB in profile, says with a certain emphatic playfulness,

*We discovered a special way of breathing for six basic emotions!!*

Musical chords. From the aria *Alba avicina*, from Puccini's *La Bohème*. Seated by the fireplace, the camera creatively and uninterrupted follows SB, who, with a certain mystery and dramatism shows the different breathing patterns. Then she says:

*But each basic emotion is also characterized by a special posture, with tension for anger and fear (she shows it). And relaxation for joy, for sexuality and for tenderness* (she shows it).

The shot only shows the fire blazing while her voice-over says, as if it were obvious:

*Each basic emotion has of course its own facial expression.*

Then we see SB with her back towards the camera and while she slowly turns her head, she says with a certain dramaticism:

*It is the ensemble of breathing, posture and face, what we have called* **Emotional... Effector... Patterns...**

And then seen in profile, she repeats in a whisper full of theatrical complicity:

*Emotional.... Effector....... Patterns.*

Abruptly the camera leaves the intimate space, and the shot is outdoors. The camera undulates over the stone walls, over the blue sky accompanied by the sound of the strong masculine gypsy lament....

> *Ay, ayii ayii ay*
> *Y hasta donde la he visto yo,*
> *Su carita llorosa*
> > *Diciendo mujer hermosa*
> > *La que tiene,*
> > *La que tiene*
> > *El español*

Now I am in the middle of nowhere, in the mountainous nature of the Andalusian Alpujarras, in a lost hera where we chose as a stage. Far behind we see the Sierra Nevada. I am seen wearing short boots, a wide skirt while I say in a very intense improvised speech that the camera records creatively:

> *Breathing ... Emotion ... The work with these emotional patterns has two main uses. One, is the possibility to induce a real emotion by having a person reproduce a special breathing pattern, as we just saw with Camila and Julián,*

The voice is heard on camera, while the face of Julian appears, first diffusely and then clearly.

> *We will now see the entire process of the emotional induction of sadness in Julian in real time, who knew nothing about this method. Because he is a Spanish actor, I will speak with him in Spanish.*

The actor is seen in the foreground as he is following the instructions given by SB in colloquial words as follows :

> *I want you to breathe in the following way: inhale through the nose in brief saccades and then exhale all the air at once through the open mouth... Yes, good, but do not blow. Now slightly lower your eyelids and frown... As you exhale feel your body become heavy, very relaxed in your body ...Let the breathing guide you... exhale as in a sigh... with a heaviness in your body ... Let the breathing guide you...*

As Julian follows the instructions, little by little his face adopts an expression of deep sorrow, until his eyes begin to fill with tears. A comment is heard on camera:

*To follow the flow of a special breathing is to enter into the emotion.*

Then after about 2 minutes of doing the exercise when the expression of sadness has become even more clear and natural, he is given the following instructions:

*Now breathe calmly, return to your normal regular breathing. Very good. Now touch your face.* It took Julian about 30 seconds to leave the emotional state, after which the following dialogue between him and SB, who was off–camera, took place:

S. What happened here?
J. Well, I had a sad remembrance.
S. Did you have any image?
J: Yes.
S: Could you tell me what the image was?
J: (pause) Well…, it is private, it was an image from the past.

The next shot is back in the threshing area; there is the sound of a waterfall and a shepherd is seen in the distance. Silence, birds chirping, stone walls, nature. SB is seen walking on the stoney ground. She slowly twirls her flowery shawl, then faces the camera saying emphatically:

*Such a procedure has strong humanistic value because it can help people to be in contact with their own emotions, and to learn to express them clearly and freely. It can also be used in psychotherapy and can help people to overcome their emotional inhibitions that are so common, especially in these present times, in our highly technological society.*

And giving a small jump and opening her arms, SB joyfully continues saying with a smile:

*The other use we can have with the same patterns is to learn to "**play** an emotion", to "control" the emotional system…, that is to say, to develop the ability to initiate and to end an emotion **at will**.*

In the foreground we see a woman, (the actress Joan Polvsen) crying desperately, until a signal to step-out is given to her. She immediately responds with an instantaneous change in breathing, her face becoming neutral. In a voice-over, SB, says:

> *Joan, a Danish actress reproduced here the pattern of sadness, the same one that was reproduced by Camila and Julian, in their case with my intention to really make them cry. This time it was used for acting, with an actress trained in the Alba Emoting method.*

SB is seen again saying, with a certain complicity with the viewer:

> *This is certainly very useful for people who need to play for example, in the theatre, or for a politician, and why not, for a salesman…*

Now we enter into the patio of a house in Lebrija, a little town in the south of Spain. I had asked permission to enter into a typical Andalusian house to film some scenes. Two elderly spinster sisters, dressed in black, opened the door for us. These characters stepped directly out of Lorca's play, *The House of Bernarda Alba*, that Pedro was co-directing and filming with a group of Danish actors.

The voice of SB is then heard as a voice-over in the next scene. She says:

> *Joan will now show you, in an exaggerated way to make it clear, how the Alba Emoting method can be used in the theater, in a scene from* The House of Bernarda Alba.

The camera shows us two women, SB and Joan, who are representing for the purposes of this film, Bernarda (SB) and Maria Josefa (Joan). In the scene, the latter approaches her mother and recites her lines, telling her why she's crying. She speaks in Danish using the weeping breathing pattern that she had learned.

Joan's dramatic declamation ends with the step-out instruction given her by Susana, still seated as the erstwhile Bernarda Alba, upon which the actress immediately straightens up, changes her breathing pattern, lifts her arms above her head, and touches her face, coming back to a neutral emotional state.

While she's doing these step-out actions, you can hear SB in a voice-over saying:

> *These actions, that comprise the step-out procedure, help the person to return immediately to a neutral emotional state. This is very necessary, especially for actors, in order to avoid what I have called "emotional hangover".*

Back on the outdoor stage, SB appears after a period of silence saying with a certain theatricality, and illustrating her words gesturally:

> *Because this is a "bottom-up" procedure, (from body to mind) based on simple, visible, physical actions, such as a particular breathing pattern, a particular posture and a particular facial expression, we can begin and end an emotion without the need to evoke complex mental, psychological triggers, as for example, images or personal memories which very often contain emotions that are ambiguous or mixed.* (There is a silent pause while the camera picks up the hills, the stones, the greenery.) Then SB continues saying,

> *Finally this method of emotional induction can be very useful in a laboratory situation to measure physiological variables such as the electrical activity of the brain, neuro-vegetative changes such as heart-rate, blood pressure, skin temperature, or even some neuro-chemical changes... manifested during a controlled emotion.*

Now we enter into a scientific experimental laboratory at the University of Oregon, in the United States. We see Susana Bloch seated while someone is placing a cap with external electrodes onto her head. The image shows her holding a magazine in her hands giving the impression to the viewer that she's sitting under a hair dryer at a hair salon, reading "Psychology Today". In a voice-over you hear:

> *This is a new system for measuring electrical brain activity, created by Don Tucker at the University of Oregon, here in the United States. We are using it as part of a research project concerning how emotions can alter brain functions.*

The next image shows us SB sitting in front of a computer typing. Then she puts her finger, like a magic wand, on the nose of a manequin on which the points where the electrodes are placed were drawn. Abruptly, as if activated by the wand, we see SB in a green dress sitting on a rock on the shore of Lake Konstanz in Germany. She is in the foreground, doing the emotional patterns of the six basic emotions in rapid succession as Pedro Sándor, who is filming, instructs her. The sequence ends with the laughter pattern which grows very big, followed by the indispensable step-out technique which shows again how instantly the emotion can be cut by a mere change in the breath.

The entire sequence was filmed and shown in real time without any editing. The lake behind and the flight of the seagulls are the only accompaniments of the different breaths.

In the next shot we are in my experimental laboratory in Paris where I am sitting in the armchair in which the physiological recordings are made. SB's voice-over explains:

> Here in Paris at the University of Pierre et Marie Curie in my laboratory at the Institute of Neurosciences, CNRS, my colleague Madeleine will explain in French some of the experiments that we are doing with the Emotional Effector patterns.

The camera shows me illustrating with gestures what my French colleague is saying in her mother tongue in a very melodious voice, and in clear and precise language.

> (The Emotional Effector Patterns also allow us to study the variations of certain physiological parameters that are activated during an emotional state. You see here the standard recording equipment used to measure these parameters in a subject in the lab. You can see the electrodes for recording muscular activity, the electrodes for recording the electrocardiogram —one on the wrist, and the other on the chest— the electrode that allows us to record the temperature of the skin and the two strain gauges that permit measurement of thoraxic and abdominal respiratory movements. All these electrodes and strain gauges are connected to a small box harnessed to the subject's back. This box is connected to a polygraph placed in another room in which all the data are recorded simultaneously.)

These recordings were done in 1989.

The camera then rapidly scans graphic images that are on the walls that the viewer perceives only as a stormy sky. It lands back again in the laboratory in Oregon at the moment that my American colleague is sitting in front of his computer viewing CAT-scan slices of the brain that were being sent from Sweden online. We were both standing with our backs to the camera that is focusing on the back of our heads as we confer while watching the screen. One hears a brief dialogue in undertones, followed by SB's, "Oh!" of surprise upon seeing the images.

The camera then immediately jumps back to the outdoor stone stage in Las Alpujarras in Spain, where I am giving my talk: the camera shows my whole figure with the hills behind while I say provocatively into the camera,

> *Obviously I will not illustrate these experimental findings with graphs and tables in a film like this because such results are better communicated in a paper. On the contrary this work with the Emotional Effector patterns and especially the process of emotional induction can only be convincingly illustrated either live, directly, or through film. This is precisely what we're doing here.*

There is another brief silence in which SB can be seen walking reflectively. She then adds emphatically, twirling her flowery scarf more vigorously:

> *I strongly believe that we must accept the observer's judgment as a valid scientific criterion especially in the study of emotions.*

The camera makes a long and slow passage over the Andalusian mountain heights, and the trees with the rays of the setting sun behind. Total silence. From a distance you see SB walking pensively. After a moment she says philosophically:

> *Discoveries can be misused. We know that from the history of science and its applications. This work with the emotional patterns has to do with something very delicate and vital, and that is the breath,* **the basis of life***! Therefore this method must be used with great care, sensitivity, and respect on the part of both the teacher and the learner.*

Next we see episodes from various workshops conducted by SB and filmed by Pedro Sándor at different times and places in the United States and Europe. At the end of these we come back again to the stone stage in Andalusia and I am seen giving a very important warning:

> *If the special breathing is correctly performed, the corresponding postural and facial elements of the effector patterns follow naturally.* **This is very important to avoid a robotic use of the method.**

While the camera says goodbye, retreating from the stone stage, traveling over the hills through the blue sky and cottony clouds, we hear again the masculine, wailing lament of the Flamenco singing from the beginning of the film, while we hear again the distant voice of SB, saying, as if from another world:

*As a cloud moves through the sky carried by the air, erotic love also has its special breath. Science, until now, has not considered this kind of love to be one of the basic emotions.* **I do**, *and Joan will show you, again exaggeratedly to make it clear, the effector pattern of erotic love…*

We see Joan in the foreground performing the effector pattern of erotic love. Her gaze becomes unfocused as her eyes are half closed. Her head tilts backwards with her neck exposed. Her arms are free and sensual. She inhales and exhales through her open mouth. And on her last out-breath, emerges from her mouth the 'ay' of the gypsy lament that sounds like it was coming from beyond the beyond…

Then we hear Susana's down-to-earth instruction to step-out, and Joan changes her breath, immediately coming back to a calm and neutral expression on her face.

The eye of the camera rises again to the sky framing two clouds that look like two winged birds approaching each other amorously… and we hear the distant voice of Susana ending with the words:

*Emotions are expressed in the breathing.*

*A human being breathing in a special way recovers the emotion.*

*Le sentiment s'exprime par le souffle et le souffle reprends le sentiment.*

One listens to the same music we heard at the beginning. We see the sky, the twilight clouds; SB, the protagonist, is seen from a distance with her back to the camera, standing close to the stone house, contemplating the faraway hillsides below. She runs her fingers through her hair in a very natural and unselfconscious way, her skirt blowing in the wind. It is like an image from the period of German Romanticism, as in some of the paintings by Gaspar Dietrich.

The camera then focuses for a long time on Susana's face, illuminated only by a candle that she holds in her hand, with a mysterious and ancestral look as if coming from the dawn of time. Everything is in a reddish glow, while in the background we hear the beginning of the love duet from Puccini's opera *La Boheme*. The eye of the camera rises again to the sky while the credits appear on the screen between the embracing clouds while the voices are singing:

—*Dammi il braccio, mia piccina...*
—*Obbedisco, signor.*
—*Che mámi di!*
—*Io t' amo*
—*Amor! Amor!, Amo...*

and ends with the love duet fading behind the mountains as if it were an echo getting lost in the infinite.

## END

An Alba Emoting Venture Production
Andalucía, España, 1990

# ACKNOWLEDGMENTS

My deep gratitude and recognition to Pedro Sándor, my lifelong friend and artistic associate who has accompanied me in this venture. His continuous advice, both complex and subtle at different stages in the writing of the original Spanish version, the innumerable and very rich discussions to clear up ideas and concepts, his constant encouragement and constructive criticisms, his artistic contribution with the creation of the filmed images, have been of incalculable value for me. Besides, Pedro has from the beginning played an essential role in the development of the *Alba Emoting* system, by projecting our laboratory experiments far beyond their mere scientific discovery, placing them in a frame of reference with human use and values, enhancing its relevance for humanity.

I also want to acknowledge the contributions of Roger Bosshard, my companion of many years, and Magdalena del Valle who both, from different domains of knowledge and at different moments in the writing of the Spanish manuscripts gave valuable support to its form and content.

And last but not least, again I thank Life who in my search for an editor for the original Spanish version brought me Isabel Buzeta: the right person, in the right moment, and in the right time.

For the present revised new English version of my book, I want to specially refer to the invaluable participation of Patricia Angelin and Elizabeth Ann Townsend. They are both actresses who learned, practiced and applied the method in their own profesion. It is thanks to their insistance that this revised version has emerged in print. For over a whole year we worked through Skype correcting errors, suggesting small changes, letting the magic of creativity emerge, always at the service of Alba Emoting and with respect to my authorship. I have invited both as my co-editors in this joint venture.

Made in the USA
San Bernardino, CA
11 January 2018